always up to date

The law changes, but Nolo is always on top of it! We offer several ways to make sure you and your Nolo products are always up to date:

 Nolo's Legal Updater

We'll send you an email whenever a new edition of your book is published! Sign up at **www.nolo.com/legalupdater**.

2 **Updates @ Nolo.com**

Check **www.nolo.com/update** to find recent changes in the law that affect the current edition of your book.

3 **Nolo Customer Service**

To make sure that this edition of the book is the most recent one, call us at **800-728-3555** and ask one of our friendly customer service representatives. Or find out at **www.nolo.com**.

4th edition

Renters' Rights:
The Basics

by Attorney Janet Portman

& Marcia Stewart

FOURTH EDITION	January 2005
PROOFREADER	Joe Sadusky
ILLUSTRATOR	Linda Allison
PRODUCTION	Jessica Sterling
INDEX	Jean Mann
COVER	Woods+Woods Strategic Design
PRINTING	Delta Printing Solutions, Inc.

Portman, Janet.

    Renters' rights : the basics / by Janet Portman & Marcia Stewart.--4th ed.

      p. cm.

    ISBN 1-4133-0150-9 (alk. paper)

    1. Landlord and tenant--United States--Popular works. I. Stewart, Marcia. II. Title.

    KF590.Z9P673 2005

    346.7304'34--dc22

                               2004065444

Quantity sales: For information on bulk purchases or corporate premium sales, please contact the Special Sales Department. For academic sales or textbook adoptions, ask for Academic Sales. Call 800-955-4775 or write to Nolo at 950 Parker Street, Berkeley, CA 94710.

Acknowledgments

Our special thanks to Mary Randolph, publisher of Nolo's Book Division, whose valuable ideas and early guidance contributed much to this book.

Many people at Nolo gave us help, information, and encouragement. Peri Pakroo, our cheerful editor, kept us efficient and upbeat; Stan Jacobsen, Erica Etelson, and Ella Hirst spent many hours doing research on the Net and in the library; Toni Ihara produced yet another colorful, creative cover; Josh Garey supplied delightful proper name puns. Jaleh Doane and Margaret Livingston have guided the book through the production process with their usual grace.

Contents

CHAPTER 3

RENT RULES

CHAPTER 4

SECURITY DEPOSITS

CHAPTER 5

DISCRIMINATION

CHAPTER 6

ROOMMATES

CHAPTER 7

REPAIRS AND MAINTENANCE

CHAPTER 8

TENANTS' RIGHTS TO PRIVACY

CHAPTER 9

HOW TENANCIES CHANGE AND END

CHAPTER 10

GETTING YOUR DEPOSIT BACK

CHAPTER 11

LANDLORD RETALIATION

CHAPTER 12

RENT CONTROL

CHAPTER 13

GETTING HELP WITH YOUR DISPUTE

APPENDIX 1

HOW TO FIND LANDLORD-TENANT LAWS ONLINE

APPENDIX 2

STATE LAWS

Introduction

Dealing with your landlord can be a challenging experience, to say the least. You may have a well-intentioned landlord who doesn't know the law or is bad with business details; or you may be up against a landlord who is mean, petty, and avaricious. (If you have a perfect landlord, you're probably not reading this book.) Perhaps you know what you *want* to do in response, but what is legal and will *work* may be something quite different.

This book gives the bottom line on your rights as a renter, including your rights to privacy; a livable home; the proper use of your security deposit; and fair, nondiscriminatory treatment from your landlord. But it's important to understand that, in many situations, you can't legally demand that the landlord live up to his legal responsibilities unless you, too, have fulfilled your duties as a tenant. For example, if you want to force your landlord to perform major repairs by using a rent withholding law, you must be current on the rent. Consequently, throughout this book we alert you to your legal duties—not to be preachy, but to educate you and prevent legal difficulties should you need to take action. Once you understand the strength (or weakness) of your position, you'll know how far you can push—both informally through negotiation and formally by invoking your legal remedies, in court if necessary. In short, our goal is to make you a savvy, practical tenant who directs just the right amount of time and energy into solving (or better, preventing) a landlord-tenant dispute.

Be warned, however, that a winning legal approach to every problem may not be possible. Even though tenants have far greater rights today than they did 25 years ago, the playing field in most states is still tilted in favor of landlords. Rental property owners have the wherewithal to hire lobbyists and lawyers to further their interests in the legislatures and courts; the efforts of a few tenant unions and consumer protection groups are often no match. And if a legal dispute spills over into court, it's often the landlord, not the tenant, who can afford an experienced lawyer.

Another note of perspective needs to be sounded. If you're dealing with an irrational landlord, you may be better off learning to live with the problem—if it's a minor one. If it's a more significant problem, you should take advantage of the first legal and practical opportunity to move on, rather than march off to court—even if the law is 150% in your favor. That's because a protracted legal battle is rarely worth the time, energy, and emotional toll it will extract. Take our word for it: Even tenants who win their lawsuits look back on their legal fight vowing never to go near a lawyer or courtroom again if they can possibly avoid it.

RENT CONTROL HEADS UP

If you live in a community with rent control, you're probably well aware of that fact (and thankful for it). It's important to understand that most rent control ordinances affect more than just the amount of rent a landlord may charge. Many of the legal principles explained in this book have a special twist when rent control enters the picture. Typically, rent control laws also regulate:

- the acceptable reasons a landlord may use for refusing to renew a lease or allow a rental agreement to continue
- the amount of notice, or warning, that a landlord must give a tenant before terminating a tenancy, and the language that must be used when writing a termination notice, and
- whether the landlord must pay interest on a deposit.

Throughout this book, you'll find rent control notes wherever it's likely that rent control will affect the main discussion. Chapter 12 is devoted entirely to rent control and explores the typical provisions in rent control ordinances in depth.

EVERY TENANT'S LEGAL GUIDE

Renters' Rights covers common problems encountered by most tenants. Each topic is discussed in more detail in the authors' larger work, *Every Tenant's Legal Guide* (Nolo). The *Guide* also covers specific environmental hazards such as lead, asbestos, and mold; landlords' liability for tenant injuries (including those caused by criminals); and permissible reasons for tenancy terminations. *Every Tenant's Legal Guide* includes an overview of the eviction procedure and tear-out forms such as a Rental Application, Receipt and Holding Deposit Agreement, Notice of Intent to Move Out, and more. For order information, see the back of this book.

Who shouldn't use this book? Don't use this book if you are renting commercial property or space in a mobile home park, hotel, or marina. If you are a tenant in government-subsidized or -owned housing (including the "Section 8" program), your lease may contain terms required by the government, which neither you nor your landlord can change. Tenants who lease residential space in condominiums are generally on the same legal footing as those who rent single-family houses, which means that this book will apply to them. However, condo tenants are also subject to the condominium's operating rules and regulations (known as "CC&Rs"), which may impose obligations or restrictions on tenants and landlords in addition to those found in federal, state, and local law.

ICONS USED THROUGHOUT THIS BOOK

TIP: A practical tip or good idea.

CAUTION: Slow down and consider potential problems.

NEGOTIATE: Strategy for dealing with your landlord.

FURTHER READING: Books, organizations, or websites that give more information about the issue discussed in the text.

RULES TO RENT BY: You'll see "Rules to Rent By" at the conclusion of every chapter. It's our way of summing up the chapter's key points. Here are a few general rules to get you started:

- **The best way to win over a prospective landlord is to be prepared.** Bringing the following information when you meet prospective landlords will give you a competitive edge over other applicants: a completed rental application, written references from landlords, and a current copy of your credit report.
- **Carefully review all the important conditions of the tenancy before you sign on the dotted line.** Your lease or rental agreement may contain a provision that you find unacceptable—for example, a restriction on guests or pets, or a ban on alterations or running a home business.
- **To avoid disputes or misunderstandings with your landlord, get it in writing.** Keep copies of any correspondence (sent return receipt requested) and follow up an oral agreement with a letter, setting out what was said (and decided). For example, if you ask your landlord to make repairs, put your request in writing and keep a copy for yourself. If he agrees orally, send a letter confirming this fact.
- **Know and protect your privacy rights.** Emotion-filled misunderstandings often arise over a landlord's right to enter a rental unit and a tenant's right to be left alone. If you understand your privacy rights—for example, the amount of notice your landlord must provide before entering—it will be easier to protect them.
- **Know your rights to live in a habitable rental unit—and don't give them up.** Landlords are required to offer their tenants livable premises, including adequate weather-proofing; heat, water, and electricity; and clean, sanitary, and structurally safe premises. If your rental unit is not kept in good repair, you have a number of options ranging from withholding a portion of the rent to pay for repairs to calling the building inspector (who can usually order the landlord to make repairs) to moving out without liability for your future rent.
- **Keep communication open with your landlord.** If there's a problem—for example, if the landlord is slow to make repairs—talk with the landlord to see if the issue can be resolved short of a nasty legal battle.
- **Make sure the security deposit refund procedures are spelled out in your lease or rental agreement.** To protect your deposit and avoid any misunderstandings, make sure your lease or rental agreement is clear on the use and refund of security deposits, including allowable deductions.

Chapter 1

Play the Landlord's Game and Win

Looking for a place? No problem—with money, great references, no pets, not too many roommates—"it's a breeze!" If your reaction to this line is, "Unfortunately, that doesn't describe me," read on. You don't have to be wealthy or squeaky clean to get the rental you want—just savvy.

The good news. Thanks to federal and state antidiscrimination laws, landlords are limited in what they can say and do when selecting tenants. Basically, unless a landlord has a legitimate business reason for turning you down, she risks running afoul of these laws, which can spell big legal trouble for her. Because antidiscrimination laws are so important, we devote a whole chapter to them: Chapter 5.

The sobering news. Aside from complying with antidiscrimination laws, landlords have a lot of leeway in choosing tenants. Landlords are legally free to chose whomever they think will be the best, most stable tenant—ideally, someone who pays the rent on time and won't cause any problems.

Since landlords can choose tenants based on their likelihood of being "maintenance-free," applicants with a shadow or two in their past (a bad reference, a few late rent payments) or a shaky present (low income relative to the monthly rent) need to know how to anticipate—and head off—the landlord's hesitations before they solidify into a "No." And if you live in a tight rental market—like New York City or San Francisco—you'll need to be fast, persistent, and street-smart to score a reasonably priced rental.

This chapter alerts you to the main factors landlords consider when choosing tenants, such as credit reports and references, and gives advice on how to improve your chances of getting a place you like—and can afford.

TENANT TRAPS

Read this chapter to find out why you should:

- **Never rent from a landlord who asks non-business-related questions or subjects you to an inquisitory grilling.** These are red flags that indicate that the landlord does not understand—or chooses not to follow—the law.
- **Never pay more for a credit check than a reasonable approximation of the landlord's actual costs.** A landlord who gouges you on this one will do the same on another occasion.
- **Never let a prospective landlord see your credit report before you do.** If the report is inaccurate, you need to take immediate steps to fix it. If the report is correct but damaging, you should prepare your explanations and defenses in advance.
- **Never lie on the rental application.** It's the kiss of death.
- **Never rent a place that you have serious misgivings about**—whether it's the landlord, the neighbors, the neighborhood, or the unit itself. It may be harder than you think to get out.

A.   Legal and Illegal Reasons for Turning You Down

A landlord is legally free to set whatever conditions he wants for a tenancy as long as they are reasonably related to his business needs and don't violate antidiscrimination laws. The Federal Fair Housing Acts (42 U.S. Code §§ 3601-3619) prohibit discrimination on the basis of race, color, religion, national origin, gender, age, familial status (having children), and physical or mental disability (including alcoholism and past drug addiction). In addition, many states and cities also prohibit discrimination based on marital status or sexual orientation. Chapter 5 discusses illegal discrimination and how to file a complaint with a fair housing agency.

A landlord may reject you for poor credit history, income that a reasonable businessperson would deem insufficient to pay the rent, negative references from a previous landlord or employer, a criminal conviction, or a prior eviction lawsuit (even one that you won). As long as he doesn't discriminate, a landlord can basically choose whomever he wants. For example, a landlord can refuse to rent to smokers or disallow pets because smokers (and pet owners) as a group are not protected by antidiscrimination laws. If your landlord's policy is no pets, no smoking, or some other legitimate lease or rental agreement term, you're out of luck unless you can make some convincing arguments for your case. (Chapter 2, Section D, suggests ways to get around landlord restrictions.)

What about roommates? A landlord can limit the number of occupants for health and safety or legitimate business reasons. A landlord may not adopt a low occupancy standard if the result eliminates families with children—this is a violation of the fair housing laws, as discussed in Chapter 5, Section A.

You are your own worst enemy if you lie on your rental application. Your landlord can easily find out that you don't make $50,000 per year by talking with your employer. Misrepresentations on the rental application are always legitimate grounds for rejection. And even if you slip by, ask yourself whether you want to rent from a landlord who is so careless. Would you be concerned to learn that the "former schoolteacher" next door is really a recently released rapist? If the landlord didn't check up on you, he probably didn't check up on your neighbor, either.

1. Rental Application Questions—How Far Can They Go?

Most landlords will want you to fill out a rental application with information on your employment, income, credit and financial information, and rental housing history and any criminal convictions. It's legal to ask for all this information and use it to make rental decisions. Landlords may also legally ask you for your Social Security and driver's license numbers and (except in New York) for proof of your legal residency in the United States. Landlords may even ask if you smoke or if you've ever been sued.

How far can landlords go? They can ask for any information that will:

- tell them whether you're likely to be a good tenant, and

- help them find you if you skip town owing them for rent or property damage.

Questions that don't relate to these two issues are probably not legal. Keep in mind, however, that not all discrimination is illegal, so some questions that may not "sound right" may in fact be legal. (See "Are You Two, Like, Together?," below.)

Look at it this way: When you rent a car, you're often asked for multiple forms of ID and your driving history. Renting a place to live isn't all that different: The landlord, as much as the car rental agency, needs to know whether you're a good risk and how to find you if things go awry. In fact, since rental property is a much bigger investment than a car, a landlord is motivated to be even pickier.

TOO EXPENSIVE? SAYS WHO?

Money talks, especially in rental housing. If the landlord reasonably concludes that you can't afford to pay the rent in view of your income and existing debt level (which he'll see on your credit report), he is not obligated to rent to you. Many landlords use a rent-to-income ratio of one-to-three (rent can be no more than one-third of your income) as a rule of thumb.

As a broad generalization, you too probably don't want to spend more than 25% to 35% of your monthly take-home pay on rent, but this will obviously depend on your other expenses. And you won't want to live in a penthouse if it means you need to eat popcorn every night.

2. Question One, Question All

While landlords are entitled to ask business-related questions on a rental application or during an interview, there is an important hitch: They should subject all applicants to the identical set of basic questions. As mentioned above, federal and state antidiscrimination laws make it illegal to single out members of certain groups (such as people of a certain race or ethnic background) for special treatment—and interview or application questions that aren't directed at everyone constitute special treatment. For example, landlords who ask about immigration history should ask all tenants, not just those whom they suspect might be in the country illegally. Questioning only those from the Mideast would amount to illegal discrimination on the basis of national origin. Similarly, requiring credit reports only from African-Americans would also be considered illegal discrimination.

Do a little background investigation of your own. If your prospective landlord is conscientious, he'll probably take the time to learn about your rental and employment history. There's no reason why you, too, can't ask a few questions to find out whether *you* want to rent from *him*. Ask current tenants and neighbors what it's like to live there; ask the tenant whose unit you're considering why she's moving out. If you learn that she's leaving in disgust over poor management or dreadful neighbors whom the landlord won't evict, you'll want to think twice about signing a lease or rental agreement. Keep in mind that a building with a large turnover rate, and especially one where evictions are common, is probably not run very well.

ARE YOU TWO, LIKE, TOGETHER?

Most landlords don't care a bit about whom you share your bed with—they're much more interested in whether you pay your rent on time and are a decent housekeeper and a considerate neighbor. Unfortunately, a few landlords see themselves as enforcers of their chosen code of morality. For instance, some people do not want to rent to heterosexual, unmarried couples, and some refuse to rent to homosexual couples.

In most states, landlords can get away with these kinds of choices. That's because unmarried straight couples and gay and lesbian couples are not protected by antidiscrimination laws except in a few states. (See Chapter 5, Section B.) This means that in most states it would not be illegal for a landlord to question you and your would-be roommate about the nature of your relationship.

If you and your friend are questioned concerning your relationship, what should you do? This is an issue for *all* roommates, even the ones who are just friends and heterosexual, whom the landlord would presumably welcome with no problem. Think about what this line of questioning bodes for future dealings with this landlord: Here is a businessperson who is inappropriately interested in his customers' private lives. Chances are he spends his time and energy checking up on his tenants' love lives, at the expense of running a pleasant and livable building. If at all possible, look elsewhere.

B. Your Credit Report Can Make or Break Your Application

For many landlords, credit reports are a litmus test that show how responsible you have been at managing money. Like it or not, your financial history is a powerful indicator of whether you will be a reliable tenant who pays rent on time and is not likely to cause problems. A landlord can legitimately turn you down for a bad credit report.

Fortunately, there are some restraints on the method of collecting and reporting on an individual's credit history. The Fair Credit Reporting Act (15 U.S. Code §§ 1681 and following) covers all aspects of credit reports, including your access to your file, your right to dispute information in it, and steps you can take to correct inaccurate reporting. It also regulates investigative background reports, including your right to be told that such a report has been requested. Some states have their own laws that give consumers more protections.

1. What's in Your Credit Report

Credit reports show your credit history for the past seven years, including whether you have ever been:

- late paying rent or bills, including student or car loans
- convicted of a crime or, in many states, even arrested
- evicted from a rental unit, or
- involved in another type of lawsuit, such as a personal injury claim.

A credit report will also state whether or not you have filed for bankruptcy in the past ten years.

If you've never borrowed money or used a credit card, the report will have large blank spaces which would normally be filled with a consumer's history. Ironically, a landlord may refuse to rent to you because you don't have a good history of debt management, even if you have been a fastidious on-time, cash-only consumer! The landlord will be worried that the first time you encounter lean times might be when the rent is due—and he has no way of knowing whether, if this happens, you'll be able to put your rental obligation at the top of your list. (See Section B7, below, for advice on how to deal with this situation.)

2. Verify Credit-Check Fees

Landlords can charge a fee for the cost of the credit report itself and
their time and trouble to order it and read it—$20 or $30 is common.
You can call the credit bureau to verify the actual cost of getting a report.
Some states regulate how much the landlord can charge (call your state's
consumer protection agency to find out if your state has set a limit). If
the landlord has charged an unreasonable amount, you can report him
to that agency.

3. Your Right to a Refund of a Credit-Check Fee

Some unscrupulous landlords collect credit-check fees but never run a
credit check, pocketing the money instead. If your landlord has done
this, you're entitled to a refund. If you suspect this illegal behavior,
contact a credit reporting agency as soon as you've been rejected by
a landlord to see whether or not the landlord actually requested your
report. If he didn't, ask for your money back; if you get no results,
contact your state's consumer protection office.

   If a credit report was ordered and you decide not to take a rental unit
or the landlord chooses someone else, you are not entitled to a refund.

4. Your Right to Know When Your Credit Report Does You In

A landlord who does not rent to you because of negative information in
your credit report is legally required to give you the name and address
of the credit agency that reported the negative information. He must also
tell you of your right to a free copy of your file from this agency.

5. Why and How to Check Your Credit Rating

Because your credit report is so important, you should always check it before you start your housing search. This will give you the opportunity to correct or clear up any mistakes, such as out-of-date or just plain wrong information. It's all too common for credit bureaus to confuse names, addresses, Social Security numbers, or employers. Especially if you have a common name (say, John Brown), chances are good you'll find information in your credit file on other John Browns—or even John Brownes or Jon Browns. Obviously, you don't want this incorrect information given to prospective landlords, especially if the person you're being confused with is in worse financial shape than you.

Looking for inaccurate information isn't the only reason to check your credit report. If your report contains accurate but damaging information, it's better that you know exactly what it says before your prospective landlord sees it. Seeing it first enables you to anticipate an objection and formulate an explanation, which will better your chances of convincing the landlord that your financial troubles are all in the past.

Copy your own credit report and save on credit check fees. If you're applying for more than one rental, you'll find that credit-check fees (at $20 or $30 a pop) mount up quickly if every landlord orders a report. Get your own credit report and make several copies to give landlords when you apply for a rental. While landlords may want to order your credit report directly (some may fear that you're doctored your copy), it's worth a try.

GET A COPY OF YOUR CREDIT REPORT

The three largest credit bureaus, with offices throughout the United States, are Experian (formerly TRW), Equifax, and Trans Union. Virtually every credit report in the U.S. is generated by one of these three agencies. They compile credit information on individuals and provide reports to landlords and others upon request. You can obtain a copy of your own credit report from any or all of these agencies.

If you'd like to see a copy of your credit report, it's about to get much easier and cheaper. The Federal Trade Commission (FTC) has approved a rule that will allow consumers to receive a free copy of their credit report every twelve months. While some states already mandate that credit reports be provided free of charge, consumers in most states currently have to pay a nominal fee (usually $8 - $9) for the report.

The FTC's ruling will force the three major credit bureaus to create a "centralized source" for accepting credit report requests. The service will be accessible via a toll-free phone number, a dedicated website, and a postal address. Because this centralized source has not yet been developed, instructions for obtaining a free credit report are not yet available.

Depending on what state you live in, you may not be able to access this service for some time. The centralized source will become available to consumers in the western United States beginning December 1, 2004, and will gradually be rolled out from west to east over a period of nine months, as follows:

December 1, 2004: Alaska, Arizona, California, Colorado, Hawaii, Idaho, Montana, Nevada, New Mexico, Oregon, Utah, Washington, and Wyoming.

March 1, 2005: Illinois, Indiana, Iowa, Kansas, Michigan, Minnesota, Missouri, Nebraska, North Dakota, Ohio, South Dakota, and Wisconsin.

June 1, 2005: Alabama, Arkansas, Florida, Georgia, Kentucky, Louisiana, Mississippi, Oklahoma, South Carolina, Tennessee, and Texas.

September 1, 2005: Connecticut, Delaware, District of Columbia, Maine, Maryland, Massachusetts, New Hampshire, New Jersey, New York, North Carolina, Pennsylvania, Rhode Island, Vermont, Virginia, West Virginia, Puerto Rico, and all U.S. territories.

You'll have to pay a fee for a copy of your report if you want more than one copy per year, but even this request will be free if you:

- receive public assistance
- are unemployed and planning to apply for a job within 60 days following your request for the report
- believe your file contains errors due to fraud, or
- were denied credit (including a place to live) because of information in your report. (You must request the report within 60 days of being denied credit or the rental.)

To request a copy of your credit report, contact any one of the credit bureaus: Experian at 888-397-3742, www.experian.com; Trans Union at 800-888-4213, www.tuc.com; or Equifax at 800-997-2493, www.equifax.com.

6. How to Handle Errors (Not Your Fault) in Your Credit Report

If you see entries in your report that are wrong, take action. Contact the reporting bureau and ask for an investigation form. On the form, list each incorrect item and explain why it's wrong. Under federal law, the credit bureau must investigate within 30 days (in some states, it's less). If the investigation confirms that you are right (or if the creditor who provided the information can no longer verify it), the bureau must delete the information from your file.

Unfortunately, a request for an investigation does not always right the situation. If the credit reporting agency fails to remove inaccurate or outdated information, lists a debt you refused to pay because of a legitimate dispute with the creditor, or reports a bogus lawsuit against you that was abandoned, you have the right to place a 100-word statement in your file, giving your version of the situation. Be sure to submit such a statement immediately if your situation fits one of the above descriptions. In addition, you can contact the Federal Trade Commission to complain about the inaccuracies. Check the government section of your phone book or call the national office at 202-326-2222.

Keep in mind that if one credit bureau has inaccurate information on you, it's likely that others do, too. If you find errors in your report from one credit bureau, be sure to check your files at the other two agencies.

7. How to Deal With Problems (Your Fault) in Your Credit Report

If your credit file shows negative but accurate information, or you have no credit history because you're a first-time renter and have never borrowed money or used a credit card, there are steps you can take to look better to prospective landlords:

- See if your landlord will accept a cosigner—a creditworthy person who signs the lease or rental agreement and agrees to cover any rent or damage-repair costs you fail to pay. Keep in mind that the landlord will evaluate the cosigner with the same criteria he used for you—so your willing but broke college buddy isn't likely to be accepted.

- Pay a large security deposit, or offer to prepay rent for several months. (Chapter 4 discusses security deposits and state limits.)

- Show proof of steps you've taken to improve bad credit—for example, enrollment in a debt counseling group, recent history of making and paying for purchases on credit, and maintenance of a checking or savings account.

- Get positive references from friends, colleagues, employers, and previous landlords.

For a detailed description of how to obtain a credit report and challenge its contents, and for information on your state laws, see *Money Troubles,* by Robin Leonard (Nolo). For suggestions on how to re-establish your good credit, see *Credit Repair,* by Robin Leonard (Nolo).

C. References Are All-Important

Your past relationships with landlords, managers, and employers can make the difference between getting a rental unit and getting rejected. Prospective landlords will usually want to talk with your current and previous landlords, your employer, and your friends. Here's what they'll typically ask.

When talking to other landlords and managers:

- Did you pay rent on time?
- Were you considerate of neighbors (no loud parties, out-of-control kids, or dangerous dogs)?
- Did you make unreasonable demands or complaints?
- Did you take good care of the rental unit?

If your landlord says you were a pain in the neck, always paid rent late, and left the place a shambles, don't expect the next landlord to welcome you with open arms.

When speaking with your boss:

- How long have you worked at this job, and how much money do you make?
- Are you a responsible person? Do you get along with coworkers?
- Do you have any serious character flaws or weaknesses?

When talking to your friends (nonrelatives):

- Are you a reliable, honest person?
- Do you have good housekeeping habits, and are you considerate of others?

A landlord can't force you to give references. And you may not want to, particularly if your current landlord or boss is a complete jerk and will have nothing good to say about you. But unless you can come up with a good substitute—another supervisor or maybe a resident manager—a prospective landlord will conclude that you're withholding the name because you're afraid of what the person might say. If you really can't come up with some names, at least have a reasonable explanation for your reticence.

Many past landlords and employers won't talk to your prospective landlord unless they have a signed release from you stating that it's okay to answer the prospective landlord's questions. In this litigious society, employers and landlords are afraid that you'll sue them for defamation or the invasion of your privacy. This written permission assures your previous landlord, current or past employers, credit sources, or personal references that you won't object if they respond truthfully to a landlord's relevant questions about your work and employment history. For this reason, many prospective landlords will ask you to sign a release.

D. Smart Moves: How to Find a Good Place

Knowing what questions landlords are legally allowed to ask and preparing for them will give you confidence as you head into your rental search. But your success will also depend on some "street smarts," not just legal know-how. Here are some proven strategies that will make your efforts more efficient and successful:

Set your rental priorities before you start looking—the rent, desired location, and number of bedrooms and whether you want to keep a pet. This will help focus your search. You don't want to drive yourself crazy running around looking at inappropriate places.

Sign up with an apartment-finding service. Expect to pay a flat fee, such as $50 to $100 for a one-month membership, providing a centralized listing of rental units for a particular geographic area. (Be aware, however, that in areas such as San Francisco and New York City, where the rental market is extremely tight, the service may well be very expensive, tied to the monthly rent of the apartment you choose.) If you have email or access to a fax machine, look for a service that will deliver daily updates of available rental units this way. Otherwise, you'll need to stop by the company's office to check out listings. Some apartment-finding services provide roommate referrals, and some agencies specialize in this exclusively—check the Yellow Pages under "Roommate Assistance" or "Referral Services."

Use your personal contacts. Get leads from people who live or work near where you want to live. Don't be shy—ask friends, coworkers, even local businesspeople with whom you have a friendly relationship. You never know who may come through with the perfect apartment—it might be the receptionist at work, your dental hygienist, or a waitress at your favorite restaurant.

Check classified ads early in the day, especially in the Sunday paper. Some newspapers issue their Sunday paper with classifieds early—even a day early. Also, many newspapers have their classified ads available online.

Work with a real estate broker or property management firm. If you're moving to a new city, these may be your best options. Be sure to check out fees. In New York City, where many property owners list their rentals exclusively with real estate brokers, you can expect to pay a fee that is tied to the rent (for example, 15% of the first year's rent) or a flat fee of $1,000 or more for a rental.

Check out university and corporate housing offices. Professors leaving on sabbatical and corporate employees who are temporarily transferred are often anxious to rent their homes for a year or more. University housing services and corporations sometimes maintain databases to help them in their leasing efforts.

Go online. Post your own "Apartment Wanted" notice on a site that permits personal messages, or check out an online rental service such as Rent.Net (www.rent.net), which lists over one million rental units.

Hit the streets. Walk or bike around the neighborhood you want to live in and look for "Apartment for Rent" signs in windows or notices on local bulletin boards. These rentals can be great finds—especially if they're not advertised in the paper, reducing the competition. If you want to live in a particular apartment building or complex but there's no sign posted, stop and talk to the manager or doorman. Get on a waiting list, if possible.

Advertise your rental search. Consider posting your own "Apartment Wanted" sign (and maybe even offer a finder's fee) in a local store, health club, or other business; or put a classified ad in a newspaper or newsletter.

Try not to compromise. If you can at all help it, don't move into a place that's a complete disaster, next to a drug house, or run by a landlord who is well known by the housing inspectors and the local legal aid office. Even if you consider it temporary, try not to settle for a questionable place. Keep looking.

Take your time. Unless you're positive that you've found your dream rental (and there are eager would-be tenants lined up behind you), don't commit yourself on the spot. Take some time, even a few hours, to think about it. Were there any little, nagging misgivings that need to be faced and resolved? For example, what about the manager's off-hand remark about his tenants' private lives that, viewed in retrospect, may spell trouble ahead? Often a return visit, or candidly sharing your doubts with a wise friend, can bring important issues to the fore. You don't want to look back later and say, "I should have seen it coming."

E. How to Impress Prospective Landlords

To gain a competitive edge over other tenants, bring a completed rental application when you first meet prospective landlords. Ask the landlord for a blank copy before you go, use the form from Nolo's *Every Tenant's Legal Guide* (by Janet Portman and Marcia Stewart), or simply bring the following information:

- Written references from landlords, employers, friends, and colleagues. If that's not possible, be sure to bring a typed list of current phone numbers and addresses. It's always a good idea to alert references to expect a call from prospective landlords. And make sure they'll speak well of you.

- A signed release from you giving permission to these references to answer the landlord's relevant questions.

- A current copy of your credit report. You can order one from any of the major credit bureaus. It usually takes about two weeks.

Be on your best "good tenant" behavior. Show up on time, dress neatly, and present yourself as someone who is both conscientious and agreeable. Realize that landlords hate dealing with overly demanding or fussy tenants who constantly complain about trivial things, so don't start off asking for a long list of improvements and special favors before you're even offered the place.

To clinch the deal on a great place, you may need to sweeten the pot—for example, by offering to pay more rent or a higher security deposit. Be aware of the possible downsides of this strategy. (See "Greasing the Wheels Can Get Messy," below.)

GREASING THE WHEELS CAN GET MESSY

If you're looking for a home in a tight rental market, you might be tempted to improve your chances over the many other applicants by offering to pay more rent, prepay rent, pay more security deposit, or do maintenance chores. Tenants have been known to barter all kinds of deals, including the offer of airline or sports tickets and attractive merchandise. If you engage in creative bribery, be aware of some realities:

- **Waiving your rights might set the stage for having them trampled in the future.** If you offer a higher security deposit than the law allows or agree to under-the-table rent in violation of a rent control ordinance, you've sent a signal that you are willing to overlook the law. If you later want to assert other rights (such as your right to basic repairs and maintenance), don't be surprised if your landlord ignores your wishes—she'll figure that if you were willing to waive legal protections once, you can be talked out of these, too.
- **Offering carrots now might make the landlord expect more.** You obviously don't want to continue to bribe the landlord every time you make a reasonable request. But once wooed, he may continue to expect "deal sweeteners." This could get expensive.

- **Choosing tenants based on the quality of their gifts is no way to run a railroad.** The best landlords are the ones who choose the best tenants—those who are responsible, considerate, and law-abiding. If you live in a multiunit building, these are the best neighbors for *you*, too. Chances are you'd rather live next door to someone who got the place because she came with great references and not because she could come up with six months' prepaid rent. Beware a landlord who hasn't learned this lesson.

RULES TO RENT BY

- **Be prepared.** Get a copy of your credit report, and check it for accuracy (and press for corrections if necessary) before your prospective landlord lays his eyes on it. Develop plausible explanations for damaging entries if possible. Get your references lined up before you start apartment hunting. Make sure that your roommates do the same.
- **Be creative.** Look for rentals in newsletters, bulletin boards, and early editions of the weekend papers and by networking.
- **Be choosy.** Don't be in a rush, and check out the landlord, the rental unit, the neighbors, and the neighborhood by asking current tenants what it's like to live there.
- **Be realistic.** Don't take on a rent that will cripple your social life or make it impossible to make other necessary expenditures.
- **Be a negotiator.** Follow our tips throughout this book on how to negotiate more favorable terms at the start of your tenancy—for example, a lower security deposit.

Chapter 2

Leases and Rental Agreements

I t's not smart for a tenant—or a landlord—to conclude rental negotiations with no more than a handshake and a promise to "See you on the first!" Especially if you've argued long and hard to get a landlord to lower the rent, bend his pet policy, promise to paint the kitchen, or add a parking spot, it's plain foolish not to ask that these understandings be written down and signed. Failing to get your rental terms on paper is the single most dangerous mistake you can make as a tenant.

On the other hand, your rental negotiations may end with the grand presentation of a lengthy lease document in seven-point type written in a language that purports to be English. It's easy for a landlord to reject you as a tenant if you won't sign on the dotted line. But signing a legal document that you don't understand is like playing chess without knowing the rules: You cannot understand whether the other side has played fair, and you cannot adjust your moves to be legal and advantageous. Signing a lease that you don't understand is the *second* most dangerous mistake a tenant can make.

This chapter discusses the key provisions typically included in leases and rental agreements and explains what to do if your landlord shies away from paper and pen. It highlights terms that are pro-tenant and those that are clearly biased in favor of landlords. It also gives some tips on how to negotiate for better terms at the beginning of a tenancy.

A. How Written Leases and Rental Agreements Differ

Both leases and rental agreements are legally enforceable agreements that establish the terms of your tenancy. As with any contract, they can be written or oral—though you should always insist on a written agreement. (See "Oral Understandings—Legal But Unwise," below.) Leases and rental agreements both cover basic issues such as the amount of rent, security deposits, and who can live in the rental unit. The primary difference between the two types of agreements is the length of the tenancy.

Before you get into the nuts and bolts of leases and rental agreements, it's important that you understand the meaning of the word "term." When you read a lease, rental agreement, or any other kind of contract, you'll come across the word "term" used in two ways:

- **As a synonym for "rule" or "condition."** For example, you may see a sentence in a rental clause that reads: "The terms of the lease include $500 monthly rent, no pets, and a duty upon the tenant to shovel the sidewalk when it snows." This means that you must pay this rent, not have a pet, and shovel that snow. If you don't do these things, you will have broken (lawyers say "breached") the agreement, and the landlord may be entitled to send you a termination notice.

- **As a way to describe the length (years or months) of the agreement.** For example, a clause may say: "The term of the lease is one year." This means that you must pay rent and abide by other rental rules for one year (and you get to live there for that length of time).

1. Rental Agreements

A rental agreement establishes a tenancy for a short period of time, usually one month. A month-to-month rental agreement automatically renews each month unless you or your landlord gives the other the proper amount of notice (typically 30 days) to end the agreement. A landlord can change the terms of a rental agreement—for example, increase the rent (unless there's rent control)—with proper written notice. In most states, this amount of notice is also 30 days. (Chapter 9 explains the mechanics of how tenancies change.)

2. Leases

A lease obligates both you and the landlord for a set period of time, usually a year. Your landlord can't raise the rent or change other terms until the lease ends. And your landlord can't force you to move out unless you breach an important term of the lease such as failing to pay the rent, or violate nuisance or other property laws by repeatedly making too much noise or damaging the rental unit. A landlord can't kick you out simply because he feels like it or is annoyed with you because you complain too much about repairs or noisy neighbors.

At the end of the lease term, you or your landlord may decline to renew it or may negotiate to sign a new lease with the same or different terms. (Landlords subject to rent control, however, often have less flexibility when it comes to deciding not to renew a lease. See Chapter 12.) Often, especially when the landlord and tenant are content with the arrangement, nobody does anything formal and the tenant stays and continues to pay rent. When this happens, in most states the tenancy will continue on a month-to-month basis, subject to the same terms and conditions, in effect converting the lease to a rental agreement. (Chapter 9, Section C, covers what happens when a lease runs out.)

3. Which Is Better—A Lease or a Rental Agreement?

Since a lease gives you more security than a month-to-month agreement, a long-term lease is usually the better option for tenants who plan to stay put for the foreseeable future. With a lease, you don't have to worry about being kicked out on short notice—unless of course you've done something bad enough to justify eviction, such as not paying rent. With a month-to-month rental agreement (except in most rent control situations), a landlord is free to sock you with a rent increase or terminate your lease even if you're a model tenant. (A landlord must, however, give you the proper notice, and cannot raise the rent nor terminate the agreement for retaliatory or discriminatory reasons. Retaliation is explained in Chapter 11; discrimination is covered in Chapter 5.)

Also keep in mind that leases don't lock you in as much as you might think. In most states, if you move out midway through a lease, your landlord can't automatically charge you for the remainder of the lease term. He must take reasonable steps to find a new tenant to take your place. As soon as the place is rerented, your obligation to pay the rent ends, and you'll have to pay only for the time between your leaving and when the new tenant moved in, plus the landlord's advertisement costs. Chapter 9, Section D, covers your rights when it comes to breaking a lease.

If you might want to move soon, you'll prefer the flexibility of a rental agreement. For instance, if you know that your job will relocate you in the near future, a rental agreement is probably your best option. Or if you're in a real pinch and are forced to rent a place you're not happy with, a rental agreement will allow you to move out easily once you find a better place.

4. Will You Have a Choice?

It's ultimately the landlord's call whether to use a lease or a rental agreement, but you may have some bargaining power. If you live in an area choked with For Rent signs or where it is difficult to find tenants for a particular part of the year—for example, a college town where most students are gone during the summer—your landlord will probably insist on a lease. That way, the landlord has the security of knowing that the unit will be generating income for him for a significant and uninterrupted amount of time.

But if you live in an area where vacancies are scarce and new tenants are easy to find, you may be offered a rental agreement. Many landlords prefer the flexibility of a rental agreement, since it allows them to raise the rent or get rid of a tenant on short notice. If a particular tenant turns out to be a good one and the landlord decides not to change the terms of the rental, the landlord will simply let the rental agreement renew month after month.

If you can convince the landlord that you'll be an excellent tenant (based on your credit history and references) and will be around for the long haul, you might be able to get a long-term lease. Wise landlords prefer to keep good long-term tenants and avoid the hassles and expenses of constant turnovers (cleaning, advertising, showing, and checking out applicants)—even if it means less flexibility in terms of increasing rent or ending the tenancy. If the landlord balks at your request for a lease, consider accepting the month-to-month arrangement for a few months and then ask again. Your track record at that point might tip the balance.

ORAL UNDERSTANDINGS—LEGAL BUT UNWISE

While many landlords want tenants to sign some kind of written lease or rental agreement, written documents aren't legally required. Oral leases or rental agreements are perfectly enforceable for month-to-month tenancies and, in most states, for leases for one year or less.

While an oral agreement is legal and enforceable, it's usually unwise to rely on one. People's memories (even yours) can become unreliable, leading to arguments over who said what and when. You don't necessarily need a five-page legal document, especially if you know and trust your landlord, but you should at least get the basic terms in writing, including the rent, the length (or term) of the rental, when and where rent is due, and any other important aspect of the understanding, such as the landlord's willingness to let you have a pet. If your landlord shies away from pens and pencils, you can put the basics on paper yourself. (Section G of this chapter, below, explains how to prepare a letter of understanding.)

B. Who Should Sign a Lease or Rental Agreement

Landlords typically want all adults (18 years of age and older) who will live in the rental unit, including both members of a couple, to sign the lease or rental agreement. Doing this makes everyone who signs responsible for all terms, including the full amount of the rent.

The landlord isn't the only one who benefits when everyone signs on the dotted line. If you have roommates, you'll want them to understand that they are bound by the landlord's rules on guests, noise, pets, and so on. As explained in "Common Legal Gobbledygook," below, it's important for everyone to realize that one roommate's serious transgression can result in the ouster of everyone.

ORGANIZE YOUR RENTAL RECORDS

This book is devoted to explaining your legal rights and how to secure them. If you're lucky, your landlord will also know the law (or will be willing and able to learn it from you). But there may be times when you'll have to press your point—in negotiation, mediation, or a court-room, if necessary.

We want to prepare you so that you'll have the maximum edge when entering negotiation or mediation, or when bringing your case to court if you need to get heavy. And the first rule in preparing a winning case is to *keep and organize essential documents.* This material will be the evidence you need to clinch your argument. Establishing a simple record-keeping system will provide a valuable paper trail should disputes develop later—for example, regarding your landlord's failure to make necessary repairs. Without good records, the outcome of a dispute may come down to your word against your landlord's, always a precarious situation. To get started right, set up a file folder for the following documents:

- a copy of your rental application, references, and credit report
- your copy of a signed lease or rental agreement
- any building rules and regulations from the landlord
- deposit information, including (if known) the location and interest rate terms of your deposit, and
- your photos and notes on condition of rental unit at move-in time.

After you move in, add these documents to your file:

- your landlord's written requests for entry
- rent increase notices
- records of your repair requests and how and when they were handled, and
- any other correspondence with your landlord, such as letters of understanding.

C. Typical Provisions in Leases and Rental Agreements

Your lease or rental agreement may be as short as one page or longer than ten. It may be typed or handwritten, easy to understand, or full of legalese. Most landlords use preprinted forms they buy in stationery stores, order from a landlords' association, or find in a software program.

Most leases and rental agreements contain "the usual suspects" of rental provisions or clauses. You'll often see them as numbered paragraphs. Unfortunately, the provisions are often dressed up in fancy legal language or buried in gargantuan sentences. This section offers plain meanings for the most common terms you'll find in a lease.

1. Names and Addresses of Landlord and Tenants

The tenant may be referred to as the "lessee" and the landlord as the "lessor." They may also be called the "parties" to the agreement. If a property manager or company is authorized to receive notices and legal papers on the landlord's behalf, you should also see that name and address.

Landlords typically want all adults who will live in the premises, including both members of a couple, to sign the lease or rental agreement. Chapter 6 provides complete details on the legal responsibilities of tenants and cotenants and related issues such as adding a new roommate. Chapter 5, Section A, discusses occupancy limits that may restrict who lives in the rental unit.

2. Rental Property Address and Details

The property address is often called "the premises." Your lease or rental agreement may also include details on any furnishings, parking space, storage areas, or other extras that come with the rental property.

3. Term of the Tenancy

The term is the length of the rental. The document should include the beginning date and whether it's a month-to-month tenancy or a lease. If it's a lease, the ending date should also be specified. Leases often have a term of one year. Section A, above, discusses the important differences between leases and rental agreements. Chapter 9 explains how tenancies end.

4. Rent

Leases and rental agreements usually specify the amount of rent due each month, when and where it's due, acceptable forms of payment, and late fees. Chapter 3 covers rent rules in detail.

5. Deposits and Fees

Expect to see details on the dollar amount of a security deposit, cleaning deposit, or last month's rent. Chapters 4 and 10 explain state laws that govern the use and return of security deposits and why it's important to know your landlord's cleaning and maintenance requirements.

6. Utilities

The landlord should state who pays for what utilities. Normally, landlords pay for garbage and sometimes for water, if there is a yard. Tenants usually pay for other services, such as phone, gas, and electricity.

7. Condition of the Rental Unit

Most leases and rental agreements include a clause in which you agree that the premises are in habitable (livable) condition and you promise to alert the landlord to any defective or dangerous condition. Chapter 7 covers tenants' important rights and responsibilities regarding repair and maintenance.

INSPECT BEFORE YOU SIGN

Always inspect the rental unit before you sign a lease or rental agreement. Think (and look) carefully before signing off on a clause that states that the rental is in fine shape. Look for damage, dirt, mildew, pest or rodent problems, and obvious wear and tear. Write down (be as specific as possible) both serious problems, such as a broken heater or leaking roof, and minor flaws such as a stained kitchen counter, dirty drapes, or faded paint. Back up your written statement with photographs.

As much as possible, try to get your landlord to fix problems before you move in. Write down any agreement in a letter of understanding as described in Section G, below.

Keeping tabs on the condition of the rental at move-in is an excellent way to protect yourself when it comes time to move out and get your security deposit returned. Without good proof of the condition of the premises at the start of the tenancy, your landlord may keep all or part of your deposit, claiming you left the place filthy or damaged it—for example, stained the rug, cracked the bathroom mirror, or left behind a broken garbage disposal. Your initial inspection (and photos) will establish that the problems existed at the start of the tenancy and are not your fault. Chapter 10 discusses how to avoid disputes over security deposits at move-out time.

Check your state statutes (listed in Appendix 2): Some require landlords to give new tenants a written statement on the condition of the rental premises at move-in time, including a comprehensive list of existing damages.

8. Tenant's Repair and Maintenance Responsibilities

A carefully written lease or rental agreement will include a statement that makes you responsible for keeping the rental premises clean and in good condition and obligates you to reimburse the landlord for the cost of repairing damage caused by your abuse or neglect. Some agreements go further and spell out specific tenant responsibilities, such as fixing clogged drains or broken windows. Many leases and rental agreements also tell you what you can't do in the way of repairs—such as painting walls or adding built-in bookshelves without the landlord's permission. Chapter 7 covers important tenant rights and responsibilities regarding repairs and maintenance, and your options if your landlord fails to provide habitable housing.

9. When and How Landlords May Enter Your Rental Unit

Many state access laws specify when landlords may legally enter rented premises—for example, to deal with an emergency or make repairs—and the amount of notice required. Some landlords include this information in the lease or rental agreement. Others are ignorant of these laws and write entry provisions that are illegal. Chapter 8 covers the landlord's right to enter rental property and tenant privacy rights, and includes a good sample privacy clause.

10. Extended Absences

Some leases and rental agreements require you to notify the landlord in advance if you will be away from the premises for a certain number of consecutive days (often seven or more). Such clauses may give the landlord the right to enter the rental unit during your absence to maintain the property as necessary and to inspect for damage and needed repairs. You'll most often see this type of clause if you live in a cold-weather place where, in case of extremely cold temperatures, landlords want to drain the pipes to guard against breakage.

11. Limits on Your Behavior

Most form leases and rental agreements contain a clause forbidding you from using the premises or adjacent areas, such as the sidewalk in front of the building, in such a way as to violate any law or ordinance, including laws prohibiting the use, possession, or sale of illegal drugs. These clauses also prohibit you from intentionally damaging the property or creating a nuisance by annoying or disturbing other tenants or nearby residents—for example, by continuously making loud noise. Leases and rental agreements may prohibit smoking.

12. Restrictions on Number of Occupants

Most landlords will set a limit to the number of people who can live in each rental unit. Landlords are not free to set unreasonably low figures (for example, two people for a two-bedroom flat) in order to maintain a "quiet atmosphere" or to reduce wear and tear. Federal law requires landlords to allow two persons per bedroom unless the landlord can point to legitimate business reasons that justify a lower number (this is difficult to do). Some states are more generous, such as California (allowing two per bedroom plus one more) and Texas and Oklahoma (which make special allowances for small children). Chapter 5, Section A, explains occupancy standards in more detail and includes advice on what to do if your landlord sets a more restrictive occupancy policy than the federal or state standard.

13. Restrictions on Use of the Property

Landlords may throw in all kinds of language limiting your use of the rental property and who may stay there. These may be minor (for example, no waterbeds, plants on wood floors, or bikes in the hallway) or quite annoying. These may be in a separate set of rules and regulations or individual clauses. Basically, your landlord can set any kind of restriction she wants—as long as it's not discriminatory or retaliatory or otherwise violates your state law. Chapter 5 covers discrimination in detail.

Some common restrictions involving pets, home businesses, sublets, and guests are discussed below. Section E, below, explains how to negotiate with your landlord on these issues.

a. No Pets

Your landlord has the right to prohibit all pets, or to restrict the types allowed—for example, forbidding dogs or cats, but allowing birds. However, a landlord may not prohibit "service" animals used by physically or mentally disabled people, as provided by the fair housing laws (discussed in Chapter 5). Many landlords spell out pet rules—for example, that the tenants will keep the yard free of all animal waste or that dogs will always be on leash.

b. No Home Businesses

Landlords may prohibit you from running a business from your home, by including a clause specifying that the premises are "for residential purposes only." The concern here is generally about increased traffic and liability exposure if one of your customers or business associates is hurt on the premises. Obviously, working at home on your computer is not likely to bother your landlord, and may not even be noticed.

If you want to run a day care operation in your rented home, your landlord may not be able to flatly prohibit it. Some states, including California and New York, are anxious to encourage family-run day care. Landlords in these states may limit the number of children, however, and any business you run must comply with state fire and health regulations regarding minimum size of the facility and fire exits.

c. No Assignments or Sublets Without Landlord Permission

Most careful landlords will not let you turn your rental over to another tenant (called "assignment"), let someone live there for a limited time while you're away (called a "sublet"), or let you rent an extra bedroom to another occupant, with you as the "landlord" (also called a sublet), without their written consent.

d. Limits on Guest Stays

It's common for landlords to limit overnight guests, such as allowing a guest for no more than ten days in any six-month period, with written approval required for longer stays. Landlords do this to keep long-term guests from gaining the status of full-fledged tenants who have not been screened or approved and who have not signed the lease or rental agreement.

14. Attorney Fees and Court Costs in a Lawsuit

Many leases and rental agreements specify who will pay the costs of a lawsuit if you go to court over the meaning or implementation of a part of your rental agreement or lease—for example, a dispute about rent or security deposits. These clauses do not apply to legal disputes that arise independently of the lease or rental agreement—for example, lawsuits over alleged discrimination.

⚠️ **Watch out for clauses that make only the losing tenant pay for the owner's lawyer's fees.** In several states, including California and New York, these unfair arrangements will be interpreted to run both ways, even though the landlord didn't intend it that way (in other words, if *you* win, the landlord has to pay your costs). A common and even-handed attorney fees clause will explicitly require the losing side in a landlord-tenant dispute concerning the lease or rental agreement—whether it's the landlord or the tenant—to pay attorney fees and court costs (filing fees, service of process charges, deposition costs, and so on) of the winning party.

15. Grounds for Termination of Tenancy

You'll often see a general clause stating that any violation of the lease or rental agreement by you, or by your guests, is grounds for terminating the tenancy according to the procedures established by state or local laws. Chapter 9 provides an overview of how tenancies end.

D. Negotiating With the Landlord

Your lease or rental agreement is probably loaded with clauses written to maximize the landlord's rights and minimize yours. That's because these rental documents are typically written by lawyers hired by landlords or their trade associations.

Don't assume, however, that every clause is written in stone. Armed with a little legal knowledge, you'll be able to figure out whether the terms and conditions of your lease or rental agreement—its clauses—are legal or illegal, subject to negotiation or not. Here's how to do it.

Knowing *when* to negotiate is as important as knowing how. Don't start bargaining the minute you see a promising rental. Take some time to establish a rapport with the landlord and give him reason to want to choose you over other applicants. Even seemingly implacable rules, especially no-pets restrictions, may melt away if the landlord likes you and wants you as a tenant.

1. Four Types of Lease Clauses

Each rental clause falls into one of four categories, depending on the issue's connection to any state or local laws on that subject. As we explain below, determining how (or whether) to negotiate with your landlord over a rental clause will depend on which category the issue fits into.

Category 1: A Restatement of Your Guaranteed Legal Rights

Many states have passed tenant-friendly laws covering key areas such as landlords' access to rental property, the amount and use of security deposits, and your right to a livable home. In addition, you may have important legal rights under federal law (particularly in the area of discrimination) and local law (especially if your community has rent control). *Your landlord cannot legally diminish these rights and cannot ask you to waive them.* This book explains which important tenant rights belong in this category, and Subsection D2, below, provides further clarification.

Your landlord is obliged to comply with tenant rights but is not usually required to inform you of them in your lease or rental agreement. A conscientious and knowledgeable landlord may relay information on tenant rights in a lease clause as a way of educating you as to how things are done.

You don't have to bargain for legal rights that are guaranteed under local, state, or federal law. If your landlord spells out guaranteed tenant rights in your rental document, fine, but you've got them regardless. So is there any reason to bring them up and ask your landlord to explicitly include your guaranteed rights in your lease or rental agreement? This might make sense if you feel you're dealing with a shifty (or ignorant) landlord. If he's merely unaware of the law, you've educated him. And if he was hoping to pull the wool over your eyes, you've disabused him of that plan.

There is, however, a risk in correcting or educating your prospective landlord. He may regard you as a troublemaker and may concoct some reason to turn you down. Since these tenant rights are yours, anyway, it may not be worth the risk of instant alienation. On the other hand, you'll learn a lot about the landlord (and whether you want to do business with him) if he reacts in horror when you mention your right to heat, hot water, and a leak-proof roof.

PLEASE, SIR, I WANT SOME MORE

Even if your guaranteed rights are specified in your lease or rental agreement, there's nothing stopping you from asking for *more*—for example, if your state sets a security deposit limit at two months' rent, you can always ask for a lower figure. Similarly, if your state guarantees you 30 days' notice before the rent can be raised, you and your landlord can agree that he'll give you 60 days instead.

Should you bargain for more favorable terms? In general, you should save your negotiating strength for the most important issues. If there is something important about your tenancy that is not even partly guaranteed under state law (such as a parking spot, which falls within Category 4, see below), save your breath for that one.

Category 2: A Variation of a Negotiable State or Local Law

Not all tenant-protection laws are off-limits to landlord tinkering, as are the ones in Category 1, above. For example, in some states a landlord and tenant may agree that the statutory notice periods for changing or ending a tenancy may be shortened if *both* agree. In California, for instance, landlords and tenants may agree to shorten the normal 30-day notice period to as little as seven days. If the rental document doesn't mention the issue, however, state law prevails.

If you see a clause that restricts rights that are given you by a state or local statute, you'll obviously need to know whether this restriction is allowed in your state—in other words, whether the rule instead fits within Category 1, above. To find out, follow the suggestions for placing your clause in the right category as explained in Section 2, below.

If your state or local law allows the landlord some wiggle room on a tenant-friendly procedure, he's allowed to take advantage of that liberty. You can't force him back to the original law. If he's stubborn, you must be prepared to offer reasons why the variation is either not necessary or not fair. You may be able to work out a compromise or offer a concession of your own in exchange for your full rights under the law. Ultimately, however, if a landlord won't budge and you feel very strongly about the issue, you'll have to look elsewhere.

Category 3: Illegal Clauses

Landlords cannot diminish certain tenant-protection laws, such as your rights to a habitable rental unit and to be free from illegal discrimination. These are the rights that fit within Category 1, above. Nonetheless, many landlords attempt to circumvent the law by rewriting it. The best example of this is when landlords try to limit their responsibility to provide habitable housing, despite the laws that exist in the vast majority of states to the contrary. Incredible though it may seem, you'll see lease clauses in which the landlord states that the premises are not warranted as fit, safe, secure, or in good repair. Most states will not uphold these clauses (Texas is a notable exception). This means that even if you sign a lease or rental agreement that contains a clause absolving the landlord of the duty to offer and maintain fit housing, you can still complain (or use a tenant remedy such as repair-and-deduct, explained in Chapter 7), and a court will not hold you to your "waiver."

A misstatement of a guaranteed tenant right isn't the only kind of illegal clause you may encounter. Some clauses are illegal because they violate an important public policy. For example, many landlords use a lease clause that states that the tenant will not hold the landlord responsible for injuries the tenant may suffer as a result of the landlord's negligence or carelessness. Most courts will not enforce these clauses because our society has decided that, for the most part, people should be held accountable for the consequences of their mistakes.

Remember that we are dealing here with tenant rights that can't be waived or diminished—in other words, they are nonnegotiable. If your landlord nevertheless attempts to avoid his responsibilities, it means that he is either unaware of your rights or deliberately violating the law. Your approach will depend on your reading of the landlord.

- **The landlord doesn't know the law.** If you think the landlord has made an honest mistake, and especially if your options as to other rentals are narrow, you may decide that it's worth pointing out to the landlord that his clause is invalid. Doing so lets him know that he's not dealing with a dummy or a pushover, and hopefully he'll be more careful in the future. There is a risk, however: You may discover that he'll do everything possible to get rid of you, preferring to rent to people who don't know their rights.

- **The landlord is deliberately violating the law.** If every sign suggests that the landlord has deliberately circumvented the law, the wise course is clear: Move on. If you don't, you can count on problems ahead.

Remain quiet and lie in the weeds. If you really need or want this rental, there is an alternate but risky approach to a shifty landlord. Knowing that the clause is illegal anyway, you may want to be silent and raise your objections when and if the issue comes up. The drawback of this tactic is that making your point after the fact can be a long and tedious process. For example, suppose you sign a lease with a clause that gives the landlord the right to throw you and your possessions onto the street if you're late with the rent (called a "self-help" eviction, such a clause is invalid in virtually every state). If you're late and come home to find your belongings on the sidewalk, you may ultimately get your tenancy back and some money damages out of the landlord to boot; but the emotional toll (and the time you spend in court) will not be worth it.

⚠ **Go along with the deal at your peril.** If you're really desperate for this rental and you think you can live with the landlord's illegal clause, you might consider keeping quiet *and* doing what the landlord has asked. For example, you may agree to pay a higher-than-legal security deposit or an exorbitant late fee. But be forewarned: Agreeing to go along with an illegal scheme has its drawbacks, as explained in "Greasing the Wheels Can Get Messy," in Chapter 1, Section E.

Category 4: A Policy or Rule Not Covered by State or Local Law

Finally, you'll see lots of lease clauses that are not regulated in the slightest by your local or state laws or court decisions. Examples include provisions for parking spaces, amount of rent (rent control excepted), rent due date, move-in date, rules regarding common area use, and procedures for registering complaints and repair requests. Some of these issues are written as clauses in the lease itself, but many are covered in "house rules," which landlords attach to leases.

But minor, day-to-day issues aren't the only ones that may be untethered to a federal, state, or local law. In some states, extremely important issues, such as security deposit limits or rules governing landlords' access to rental property, are not governed by law. For example, New York and Texas do not limit the amount of security a landlord may demand. Clearly, before sounding off with a haughty demand to reform an "illegal" clause, you'll need to know whether your state law does, in fact, regulate the issue. (Section 2, below, suggests ways to correctly place your clause.)

Issues that aren't governed by law are the truly negotiable ones. Here you are both free to bargain, restrained only by the strength of your position. If it's a renters' market and the landlord's property is littered with Vacancy signs, you can expect more cooperation than if there are 17 professional couples lined up waiting to take the unit with no demands. Rather than push now for a better deal, it sometimes makes sense to get the rental and then, after you have established yourself as a stable, desirable tenant, ask the landlord to revisit the issue and possibly change that lease clause. Changing rental agreements and leases is covered in Chapter 9.

2. Placing a Clause in the Right Category

It's one thing to understand that lease clauses run the gamut from correct restatements of guaranteed legal rights (Category 1) to permissible variations on tenant rights (Category 2) to downright illegal provisions (Category 3) and, finally, to issues that aren't governed by law (Category 4). But before you can plan a negotiation strategy, you need to understand where a *particular* clause belongs. For example, suppose Clause 10 of your lease states that the tenant agrees to allow the landlord to enter the rental property with no notice. Are there any laws that protect rental privacy in your state? If not, it's a Category 4 issue and there's nothing you can do but bargain for a more considerate arrangement. But maybe your state does regulate the times and manner in which a landlord may enter and doesn't allow the landlord to deviate from this scheme. If so, that clause belongs in Category 3. Yet again, if the landlord and tenant *are* allowed to bargain over this issue, it's a Category 2 matter.

In order to find out where a particular clause falls, you'll need to read about the issue first, by turning to the appropriate chapter in this book. To continue with our privacy example, you'd turn to Chapter 8, "Tenants' Rights to Privacy," to learn about the ways that states do (and don't) protect tenant's privacy. Then, you'd turn to the chart in Appendix 2, "State Laws on Landlords' Access to Rental Property," to see whether your state has a law (statute) on the subject. If it does, you'd be well advised to read that statute. (In Appendix 1, we show you how to access your state statutes online.) Many times, lawmakers want to make sure that the law is understood as Category 1—no variations allowed—and say so right in their statute.

We don't pretend, however, that it's always easy to find out where a clause belongs in our four-part scheme. A lot of landlord-tenant law isn't in statutes at all, but instead in law that is made in court cases and written down by judges in court opinions. And even when there is a statute on the subject, you may have to read court decisions to find out whether it's okay for landlords to vary the rules (Category 2).

A useful short-cut to properly categorizing a lease clause that concerns you is to contact your local tenants' rights group or state consumer protection agency for a specific answer. A good rule of thumb is that the more important the issue, such as habitability, the more likely it is to be an iron-clad, Category 1 matter. Less important matters, such as amount of notice to change or end a tenancy, are more apt to be open to bargaining (Category 2). And there are several big-ticket issues, such as discrimination, avoiding responsibility for injuries, and physically evicting you without first going to court, that are downright illegal (Category 3) in virtually every state.

3. Concluding Your Negotiations

Negotiation with your landlord should always end with a written version of what the two of you agreed to. For example, if he has agreed to omit an illegal clause, cross it out and make sure that both of you initial and date the cross-out. Similarly, add signatures and the date if you add a clause to a preprinted lease or rental agreement. If your landlord offers to fix the oven or install security bars on the windows, write this into the lease or rental agreement and set a deadline for work to be completed (ideally, before you move in). Or outline the terms of your agreement in a letter of understanding. (See Section G, below.) Negotiation techniques are covered in more detail in Chapter 13.

E. Common Negotiation Issues

This section discusses some common issues you may be able to negotiate—pets, guests, home businesses, and roommates. Often, an offer to pay more rent or a higher security deposit will convince a reluctant landlord to modify her policies.

Other chapters provide specific advice on negotiating on

- rent increases and late rent (Chapter 3)
- deposits (Chapter 4), and
- breaking a lease (Chapter 9).

1. Pets

Several humane societies across the country offer pet-owning tenants helpful materials on how to negotiate with a landlord who doesn't normally allow pets. One particularly successful program is Project Open Door of the San Francisco Society for the Prevention of Cruelty to Animals (SPCA). For more information, contact the San Francisco SPCA at 2500 16th St., San Francisco, CA 94103, 415-554-3000. Also, *Dog Law*, by Mary Randolph (Nolo), includes a chapter on how to negotiate a lease and other issues of interest to pet-owning tenants.

2. Guests

As mentioned earlier, some leases limit guest stays. If you plan on having regular guests—for example, your college roommate stays with you two weekends a month when she's in town on business, or your boyfriend sleeps over a few nights a week—you'll need to think about how to handle this issue. If your landlord lives far away and doesn't have a resident manager, you may decide to take a chance that you'll never be found out. You might get away with it if you're always current with the rent and have no hassles with other tenants. (Be assured that when a disgruntled neighbor complains about you to the landlord, the first words out of the neighbor's mouth will be a description of your boyfriend's overnight stays, even if these visits have nothing to do with your problem with the neighbor.) But if the landlord lives downstairs, ask her to revise this clause. Perhaps you can compromise by offering a little more rent. If she resists unreasonably, consider looking for another rental.

3. Home Businesses

If you are one of the over 20 million Americans who run a business from your house or apartment, make sure your lease or rental agreement doesn't specify that the premises are "for residential purposes only." If you're working alone or your job primarily consists of making phone calls or using your computer, you've probably got nothing to worry about (and landlords in California may not prohibit tenants from operating a licensed child care facility). But if clients or deliveries will be coming on a regular basis, you'll want to discuss the issue with your landlord, who may be concerned that neighboring tenants may be inconvenienced. Where will your visitors park, for example? Will your piano students disturb the neighbors?

A landlord who does allow you to run a business from your rental unit may require that you maintain certain types of liability insurance. (In California, however, landlords cannot insist that tenants who operate licensed child care facilities obtain insurance.) That way, the landlord won't wind up paying if someone gets hurt on the rental property—for example, a business customer who trips and falls on the front steps. If you can obtain a quote for liability insurance before approaching the landlord, obviously your chances of an official okay go way up.

Also, be aware that if you use your residence as a commercial site, the property may need to meet the accessibility requirements of the federal Americans With Disabilities Act (ADA). For more information on the ADA, contact the Department of Justice, Office on the Americans With Disabilities Act, Civil Rights Division, in Washington, D.C., at 202-514-0301.

Finally, even if it's okay with your landlord, your home-based business may violate local zoning laws governing the type of businesses allowed (if any) in your residential neighborhood. The ordinances are often vague as to the type of business you can operate—for example, many allow "traditional home-based businesses," but don't provide a more specific definition. However, these laws are often quite detailed as to the following issues:

- restricting the amount of car and truck traffic the business can generate
- barring outside signs
- prohibiting employees or at least limiting their number, and
- setting a limit on the percentage of the floor space that can be devoted to the business.

4. Roommates

Landlords may set reasonable limits on the number of persons who will live in a rental. (See Section C, above.) A landlord who limits your occupancy to the federal standard of two per bedroom (or the state limit, whichever is higher) is within her rights. Even if the rooms are big, you will have a hard time finding legal support for a higher number of occupants. But you may be able to convince a landlord to allow more tenants if you offer to compensate for the additional wear and tear that higher numbers of occupants cause. You might offer a higher security deposit (assuming the deposit is not already at the state maximum) or even a higher rent.

SMOKE GETS IN YOUR EYES (AND DRAPES)

Landlords increasingly prohibit smoking in individual rental units as well as common areas. The reason: Smoking damages carpets, drapes, and paint, thus increasing the landlord's maintenance costs. A blanket prohibition on smoking is not illegal.

   If you want to smoke in a declared smoke-free building, consider offering a higher security deposit which will cover expected refurbishing costs. This may assuage your landlord's worries. This avenue may be foreclosed, however, if your state regulates security deposits and it's already at the state maximum. And keep in mind that the landlord may not be able to give in to your request without violating his promises to other tenants: If a building has one ventilation system or windows that freely communicate air, allowing one tenant to smoke impinges on all, thereby destroying the smoke-free nature of the building which other tenants doubtless jealously guard.

COMMON LEGAL GOBBLEDYGOOK

Here's the real meaning of some legal terms you may see in a lease or rental agreement.

Committing waste. This means seriously and intentionally damaging the property—something your lease or rental agreement will probably prohibit.

Hold harmless. Many form leases include a provision that attempts to absolve ("hold harmless") the landlord in advance from responsibility for all damages, injuries, or losses, including those caused by the landlord's misdeeds. Such pro-landlord language is blatantly illegal. If your landlord assaults you, or you're injured because of a dangerous or defective condition the landlord knew about but failed to fix in a reasonable time, no boilerplate lease provision will protect your landlord from civil and possibly even criminal charges.

Indemnify. This one usually accompanies the "hold harmless" clause. It means that if the landlord is sued or has to pay money for something you are responsible for, you agree to pay his costs. For example, if another tenant trips on the skateboard you've carelessly left on the stairwell and sues both you and the landlord, you agree to pay the landlord's legal fees if a jury decides that you were at fault. It is not illegal to agree to indemnify your landlord.

Joint and several liability. Many leases and rental agreements state that all tenants are "jointly and severally" liable for paying rent and abiding by terms of the agreement. This bit of legalese means that each tenant is legally responsible for the whole rent, and that the misdeeds of one tenant—for example, keeping a pet in violation of a no-pets clause—will allow the landlord to evict all of you. Cotenants are jointly and severally liable even if the lease doesn't say so. (See Chapter 6, Section A, for a complete explanation.)

Liquidated damages. This item is often found in fixed-term leases. It means if you move out before the lease expires, you are supposed to pay the landlord a predetermined amount of money (damages) for his loss of rent caused by your early departure, irrespective of the amount of rent money that the landlord actually lost when you stopped paying rent. Usually landlords set the amount of liquidated damages at the entire security deposit or many hundreds, or even thousands, of dollars in addition to the deposit. In some states, liquidated damages clauses are unenforceable—which doesn't mean that you can take off scot-free, just that you will be liable only for the landlord's actual damages, which he must prove in court.

Quiet enjoyment. You have a right to live undisturbed, free from disturbance from your landlord or neighboring tenants whom he has failed to control. Your landlord must not act (or fail to act) in a way that seriously interferes with your normal use of your home—for example, by allowing garbage to pile up or failing to correct a neighboring tenant whose constant loud music makes it impossible for you to sleep.

Validity of each part. Leases and rental agreements commonly include what lawyers call a "savings" clause, which means that, in the event that one of the other clauses in the lease or rental agreement is found to be invalid by a court, the remainder of the agreement will remain in force. Given the number of blatantly illegal clauses that lots of landlords stick in their agreements, it's not hard to see why they need this one.

F. Signing a Lease or Rental Agreement

At the end of the lease or rental agreement, there will be space to include your landlord's signature, street address, and phone number, or that of the person she authorizes to receive legal papers, such as a property manager. There's also space for your and other tenants' signatures and phone numbers, as well as any cosigner (someone who agrees to cover any rent or damage-repair costs you fail to pay).

If your landlord has altered a preprinted form by writing or typing in changes, be sure that you and the landlord initial and date the changes when you sign the document.

Make sure you sign the lease or rental agreement at the same time as the landlord and that you get a copy then and there. This assures both sides that no changes can be made after only one party has signed.

G. Get It in Writing: A Letter of Understanding

Some landlords don't want to bother with a written lease or rental agreement. Others provide a rental document that is unclear on key issues such as the circumstances under which the landlord may enter the rental unit. And some won't want to take the time to add clauses or promises that the two of you have negotiated. In any case, you don't have to settle for the hope that the two of you will remember precisely what agreement you made. There's a way to nail down an oral understanding that lawyers use all the time. It's called a "letter of understanding."

Here's a general overview of how it's done. We suggest specific ways to use a letter of understanding in later chapters. After you and the landlord have reached an agreement concerning basic terms—rent, deposits, repairs—write down that understanding in a letter to the landlord. At the end of the letter, ask him to respond if he feels you have misunderstood or misrepresented your agreement. Hand-deliver your letter or, better still, mail it return receipt-requested. Keep a copy of the letter and the post office receipt in a safe place. A sample letter of understanding is shown below.

What good does this do you? Let's say there's a dispute over an issue covered in your letter and the two of you end up in court. When you show the judge the letter and the receipt, in most states the judge will presume that your landlord received your letter *and agreed with your version* unless he promptly wrote back and argued otherwise. If the landlord disputes your version for the first time in court, he'll be starting with a serious handicap when it comes to convincing the judge that he's right.

Letters of understanding are useful in any situation where you will be relying on your landlord's (or anyone else's) oral promise. For example, suppose that you buy a clothes dryer after the landlord promises that he'll install a hook-up. If he reneges on his promise, you'll be stuck with the dryer. Without your letter of understanding safely tucked into your rental papers file, you'll have a hard time persuading a judge that the promise was made. Chapter 13 covers disputes and small claims court.

SAMPLE LETTER OF UNDERSTANDING

August 24, 200X
Ms. Iona Lott
68 Seventh Avenue
Rockyport, Maine 12335

Dear Ms. Lott,

Thank you very much for agreeing to rent me apartment #4 at 68 Seventh Avenue. I understand that you will lease the apartment to me for $750, due on the first of every month, starting September 1, 200X, and ending on September 1, 200X. Thanks for including the parking spot and allowing me to bring my dog Ruff. When I move in on September 1, I'll have the $750 security deposit that you asked me to bring, along with the first month's rent.

If your understanding of our agreement differs from mine, please let me know as soon as you receive this letter. If I don't hear from you by August 30, I'll assume that I have noted these details correctly. I look forward to moving in on the first.

Yours truly,
Izzy Real, Tenant
1236 Williams Avenue
Rockyport, Maine 12335
207-555-4567

MORE INFORMATION ON LEASES AND RENTAL AGREEMENTS

Questions about a lease term or clause

If you run across terms or whole clauses not discussed here, get more information before you sign the lease or rental agreement. Tenants' rights groups, which exist in many areas, will be able to answer your questions. Or, if you're signing a long-term lease for a valuable property, you may want to see a lawyer.

Questions about state law

The charts in Appendix 2 contain summaries of essential landlord-tenant laws. In addition, a few states require that specific information be included in leases and rental agreements, such as details on where security deposits will be held and interest payments or specific disclosures regarding the condition of the property. Check your state statute. (Appendix 1 provides a brief overview of legal research.)

Where to complain about illegal or questionable clauses

If you think a clause is illegal, check Appendix 2 to see whether your state has a statute that covers the issue. Contact your state's consumer protection or attorney general's office for landlord-tenant information.

Where to find model leases

Nolo has developed lease and rental agreement forms that are clearly written and fair to both landlords and tenants. When you use them in conjunction with the accompanying state-specific information, your document will be legal in every state. Forms (on paper and on disk) are available in *Every Landlord's Legal Guide,* by Marcia Stewart, Ralph Warner, and Janet Portman. Also, Nolo's small book, *Leases and Rental Agreements,* by the same authors, has tear-out forms. Finally, *LeaseWriter,* a Nolo software program, will guide you to creating state-specific leases and rental agreements. For order information, see the back of this book.

RULES TO RENT BY

- **Get it in writing.** If the landlord won't offer a written lease or rental agreement, use the next best thing: a letter of understanding.
- **Cover the essentials.** Make sure you're clear on the key issues before you sign on the dotted line: rent (how much, when, where due, and how it's paid), deposits (the amount, use, and return policy), roommates, pets, and parking.
- **Understand what you sign.** Never sign a legal document without understanding what it means. Refer to this book, a tenants' rights organization, or an experienced friend or attorney if you aren't sure.
- **Know the difference between a lease and a rental agreement.** Bargain for the one that suits your situation.
- **Watch out for illegal lease provisions.** Understand your state law so that you will know them when you see them.

Chapter 3

Rent Rules

For most tenants, "What's the rent?" is the first question to ask when considering a rental. Little wonder, since it takes the biggest chunk of your hard-earned income. Rent is first on your landlord's list of essentials, too. The rent you pay each month probably covers his mortgage, operating costs, the payments on his Winnebago, and his kid's braces. If you pay on time, your landlord will be happy. If you're late, you can count on trouble.

This chapter summarizes your key rent rights, and Appendix 2 provides citations for your state rules on when rent is due, the amount of notice required to change or end a tenancy, security deposits, and more. Tenants who live in a city with rent control such as New York City, Los Angeles, San Francisco, and Newark enjoy far more protections and rights than those in most of the other states.

GET YOUR RENT CONTROL ORDINANCE AND READ IT

If you live in an area covered by rent control, it is essential that you get the ordinance and become familiar with it. Typically, rent control ordinances cover more than just the amount of rent that a landlord can charge—they often regulate security deposits (such as requiring interest) and the allowable reasons for a tenancy termination. If your city has a rent control ordinance, it should also have a rent control board which can provide you with a copy of the ordinance. The state charts in Appendix 2 list cities with rent control laws. (For more on rent control, see Chapter 12.)

A. Rent Gouging: Isn't There a Law Against It?

There's a short answer to this question: No, unless you've got the protections of rent control. The more popular the area, the more you can expect to pay. You can always try to negotiate on rent, but if there's lots of competition, you probably don't stand much of a chance. In fact, it might be to your advantage to offer more than the advertised rent to clinch the deal.

It's perfectly legal for a landlord to set a higher rent in response to competition. It is not legal, however, to:

- Advertise a certain rent and then demand a higher one. This is a variation on the old "bait and switch" game and is illegal under federal and state law. If you encounter this tactic, contact the consumer protection division of your local prosecutor's office.

- Quote a higher rent based on your race, sex, or other group characteristic. If you feel the landlord is discriminating against you by charging more than the advertised price, see Chapter 5 for advice.

B. The Nitty-Gritty on Where and How to Pay Rent

Your lease or rental agreement should spell out the details on when rent is due and where and how to pay it. If these important items aren't covered in your tenancy agreement, be sure to clear them up with your landlord before you move in. (Write a letter of understanding, as explained in Chapter 2, Section G.) As with most rental issues, your landlord calls the shots on these things. It doesn't hurt to negotiate, however, if you really prefer a different rent due date or form of rent payment.

1. Rent Is Usually Due the First of the Month

Most leases and rental agreements call for rent to be paid monthly, in advance, on the first day of the month. However, landlords are normally legally free to establish a different monthly payment date—or even to require that rent be paid weekly or bi-monthly. Some landlords make the rent payable each month on the date the tenant first moved in. Most find it easier, however, to prorate rent for a short first month and thereafter collect rent on the first of the month.

2. Expect to Mail Your Rent Check to Your Landlord

Your lease or rental agreement probably also states where you should pay the rent and how it should be paid. Mailing it to the landlord's business address is the most common method of rent payment, unless your landlord or manager has an on-site office. If you mail your rent check, make sure that it arrives on the due date. It is not sufficient to mail your check on the day it is due.

Tenants often feel that the form of payment—cash or check—should be up to them. Unfortunately, it's not your call. Just like restaurants and shops, landlords are legally free to insist on a particular form of payment. Most require rent be paid by check or money order, but some landlords now allow payment by credit card (a great way to build up frequent flyer miles!) or automatic debit (rent payments are debited automatically each month from your bank account and transferred into the landlord's account).

These days, many landlords won't accept rent in cash—they don't want the risk of keeping large amounts of cash on hand. Your safety, too, will be imperiled if the word gets out that you regularly make a trip to the manager's office carrying several hundred dollars in cash. If you must pay in cash, be sure to get a written, dated receipt stating your name and the amount paid. It's your only proof that you did, indeed, pay the rent.

C. Mabel, Isn't There a Grace Period?

Lots of tenants are absolutely convinced that if rent is due on the 1st, they actually have until the 5th (or sometimes the 7th or even the 10th) of the month to pay, because they are within what they believe to be a legal grace period. Sorry, but this is not true. Rent is legally due on the date specified in your agreement.

The only exception is when the rent due date falls on a weekend or legal holiday. Most lease and rental agreements state that when the rent due date falls on a weekend day or legal holiday, the tenant must pay rent by the next business day. This sensible practice is legally required in some states and is the general practice in most. If your landlord insists on receiving the rent check by the first of the month (or other due date), even if mail is not delivered on that day, take a look at the law in your state—you may find that your landlord is violating it. If not, you may have to bite the bullet and get your rent in early.

What will happen if you don't pay on time? Usually, your landlord will:

- send you a note or pay you a visit, demanding the rent
- begin assessing late fees if there is a late fee provision in your lease or rental agreement, and
- send you a termination notice, telling you that if the rent is not paid within a certain number of days or if you haven't moved out by then, he'll begin eviction proceedings.

Laws in a few states restrict the imposition of late fees, both by amount and whether the landlord must wait until you're a certain number of days late before he imposes them. Likewise, some states make the landlord wait a few days before sending a termination notice. But if you've been late with the rent before, some states allow the landlord to terminate immediately. (Section F, below, covers evictions for nonpayment of rent in more detail.)

D. What to Do—and Not to Do—If You Can't Pay Rent on Time

Rare is the tenant who's never had a problem paying rent on time or in full. If you are a conscientious and honest tenant who is temporarily short on funds, most landlords won't evict you for paying rent a little late one month. You're more likely to be successful by being up-front about your situation and asking for an extension, rather than simply not paying rent (or sending a rubber check). Expect to pay a late rent fee if your lease or rental agreement has this provision, and don't press your luck with another request to pay late soon.

This section covers the dos and don'ts of paying late. The following sections discuss the consequences of being late—specifically, late rent fees and tenancy terminations.

1. Don't Ignore the Problem and Hope It Will Go Away

If you can't pay the rent on time, you may be tempted to hope the landlord won't notice—after all, she's got many tenants to keep track of, and one late check will hardly be noticed, right? Wrong. Remember, it's likely that your landlord is counting on your timely check to cover her own mortgage payment. Because the bank won't forgive her tardiness, she can't afford to ignore yours. And it's equally naive to think that you can ignore the landlord's phone calls or notes or think that she will swallow ridiculously lame excuses.

2. Never Send a Check You Know Will Bounce

Nothing infuriates a landlord more than dealing with a sneaky tenant who consistently bounces rent checks. Stirring up your landlord's ire isn't the only consequence of a bad check: Keep in mind that sending a worthless check (or one that's not signed) is like sending no rent at all. If your landlord has a late fee policy, it will kick in regardless of your bounced check; and, if the landlord chooses, he can also terminate your tenancy. Rubber checks buy no time.

Like any other business, your landlord has the legal right to charge you if your rent check bounces. The charge must be reasonable—such as the amount the bank charges for a returned check, probably $10 to $20 per returned item, plus a few dollars for the landlord's trouble.

Your landlord should tell you in advance—in the lease or rental agreement, orally, or by means of an obvious sign in the rental office where you bring your monthly check—that a bounced check fee will be imposed.

Negotiate a partial or delayed rent payment. A landlord who considers you a good tenant won't want to lose you, since it's often difficult and expensive to evict you, then find and move in good tenants. This means you can probably get the landlord to accept a portion of the rent now—maybe even a small portion—and the rest later. Here are some basic steps to take:

- Ask your landlord in writing (as far in advance as possible) for a few extra days.

- Explain your difficulties and emphasize (if you can) that they are only temporary.

- Offer (if at all possible) to pay at least some of the rent on time.

- Give your landlord written assurance of your plan to pay the full rent by a certain date, such as the 15th of the month—and make sure you keep your promise.

- Explain that the problem won't happen again and that you'll pay your rent on time in the future.

- Be prepared to pay a late fee if the landlord has a late fee policy. Or, if you think your landlord will be responsive and your late rent is a rare occurrence, see if you can get him to forgo a late fee.

E. Late Rent Fees

Landlords often impose a late fee when rent is even a few days late. But the size of the late fee is subject to legal limits, and in some situations it's not legal to impose one at all.

1. Are Late Fees Legal?

If your lease or rental agreement says nothing about late fees, your landlord may not impose one, no matter how reasonable it is. For example, if you hand your rent check to the landlord two days late and he tells you he will accept it only if you pay an additional $10, you may refuse unless your lease or rental agreement includes a late fee clause. Keep in mind, however, that being too hasty to assert your rights over a relatively modest sum of money may not be worth the bad feelings that could come back to haunt you in the future.

2. Limits on Late Fees

Most states do not put dollar limits on late fees. Does this mean your landlord can charge whatever he wants? No. Under general legal principles, your landlord may not charge an unreasonably high late rent fee.

Here are some guidelines for judging what's unreasonable:

• The fee shouldn't begin immediately. Normally, a late fee should not apply until at least three days after the rent due date.

• The fee should be within a certain percentage of your rent. Your landlord is always on shaky ground if the late charge exceeds 5% of the rent. That's $38 on a $750-per-month rental. Of course, if the rent is extremely late—say, ten days—a higher late fee, such as 10% of the rent, might be reasonable.

3. What to Do About Excessive or Questionable Late Fees

Obviously, the surest way to avoid a late fee is to pay your rent on time. But if you cannot do this, don't automatically assume that there's nothing you can do about the penalty.

a. When There's No Provision on Late Fees

Your landlord may not impose a late fee unless the lease or rental agreement has a late fee clause (or unless he's told you about the policy, if you have only an oral rental agreement). However, this rule of law won't stop some landlords.

If you refuse to pay the fee, be prepared to be asked to move at the first legal opportunity—with proper notice if you rent with a rental agreement, or by the landlord refusing to renew your lease when it expires. Remember, in most states a landlord can terminate a month-to-month tenant, or decide not to renew a lease, without having to give a reason. (If you live in a state that prohibits landlord retaliation, discussed in Chapter 11, you may have some protection, but you're still in for a legal fight.) To avoid the risk of losing your home, if the amount is something you can live with it may make more sense to pay the fee and begin looking elsewhere for a better landlord.

b. When You've Agreed to an Outrageously High Fee

If you've signed a lease or rental agreement that contains an outlandish late fee policy, you can still refuse to pay it and challenge it in court when the landlord seeks to evict you for breaking a lease provision. Why? Most courts consider the imposition of enormous late fees, like outrageous high-interest loans, to raise an important public policy issue. They will listen to your defense (though not necessarily rule in your favor) in spite of the landlord's claim that you "waived" the right to protest when you signed the lease or agreement. (If you've stayed with us since Chapter 2, Section D, you'll recognize this type of clause as a Category 4 illegal clause.)

We suggest, however, that you not risk the threat of an eviction lawsuit (which always includes the possibility that you'll lose). Instead, pay the fee if possible and file your own lawsuit in small claims court, asking that the judge order the landlord to return it. (Small claims court is covered in Chapter 13.) That way, the only thing at stake is your time and the small filing fee, not your home. But it goes without saying that once you've sued your landlord you can expect a termination notice at the first legal opportunity, and would do well to begin checking the classifieds for a new rental.

F. Tenancy Terminations for Nonpayment of Rent

If you are late with the rent, landlords in most states can immediately send you a termination notice giving you a few days in which to pay up or move before the landlord can file for eviction. These are usually called Pay Rent or Quit notices—you are given a few days to pay or move out ("quit"). If you do neither within the time limit, the landlord may then file an eviction lawsuit against you. The rules vary widely among states, including:

- **How soon landlords may serve a Pay Rent or Quit notice.** While most states allow landlords to send the notice the first day the rent is late, a handful don't let the landlord send the notice until you're a certain number of days late.

- **How the notice must be served.** Some states require the landlord to serve the notice personally; most states allow mailing.

- **How quickly you must pay the rent before the landlord can terminate the tenancy.** In most states, landlords must give the tenant three to five days to pay up or face a termination. But some states don't give you any time at all. Instead, if you fail to pay rent on time—even just once—the landlord can simply demand that you leave, with what's called an Unconditional Quit notice.
- **What happens if you're late more than once.** In many states, if you're late with the rent a second or third time within a specified number of months, the landlord doesn't have to give you the usual few days to pay—she can terminate the tenancy immediately, the moment the rent is late, with an Unconditional Quit notice.

Eviction itself—that is, physically throwing you and your possessions out of the property—can't be done until the landlord has gone to court and proved that you've done something wrong (like not paying the rent) that justifies eviction. For a discussion of the eviction procedure, including time periods, negotiation strategies, and an overview of an eviction lawsuit, see *Every Tenant's Legal Guide,* by Janet Portman and Marcia Stewart (Nolo).

G. Rent Increases

Rent increases are an inevitable part of any tenant's life. In most areas without rent control, there is no limit on the amount your landlord can increase the rent. But landlords cannot raise the rent at whim. The timing of a rent increase, and the way your landlord communicates it, are governed by statute in most states.

Also, in most states landlords cannot increase rent in retaliation after you exercise specified legal rights guaranteed to tenants, and cannot illegally discriminate in their system for raising rent.

1. When and How Your Landlord Can Raise the Rent

Except in cities with rent control, your landlord's legal right to raise the rent depends primarily on whether you have a lease or a month-to-month rental agreement.

If you have a lease, your landlord can't raise the rent until the end of the lease period, unless the lease itself provides for an increase or you agree to it.

If you rent under a month-to-month rental agreement, the landlord can raise the rent (or change any other term of the rental arrangement) by giving you the proper amount of notice, which in most states is 30 days. Also, the rent increase notice must be in writing; in some states, certified mail is required. Oral notices are ineffective in most states and, unless you specifically agree to the rent increase, you are not obligated to pay it.

2. Effect of Rent Increase on Security Deposit

Rent increases often trigger security deposit increases. Here's how it happens: Many states limit the amount a landlord can charge for a security deposit. Typically, deposits are capped as a multiple of the monthly rent—for example, the maximum deposit may be twice the monthly rent. But this means that if the rent has gone up legally, the security deposit may also be legally increased. For example, if the deposit is twice the monthly rent, and your $500 rent has gone up to $550, the deposit limit rises from $1,000 to $1,100. (See Chapter 4 for more on security deposit increases.)

3. Responding to an Illegal Rent Increase

What should you do if your landlord doesn't give you proper written notice for a rent increase?

If you're a month-to-month tenant and it's not that big a deal, you're better off going along rather than insisting on your rights and facing a chill in your relationship. (Besides, since the landlord can "do it right" with typically 30 days' notice, your objections will only buy you one month's time.) It's usually a good idea to put the increase in writing, so that the amount of the increase can't mysteriously grow. Ask the landlord to prepare a new lease or rental agreement confirming the new arrangement or write a letter yourself confirming the new terms. (See Chapter 2, Section G, on letters of understanding.) As with all correspondence, be sure to keep a copy in a safe place with your other rental papers.

It's a somewhat different situation, however, if you have a lease. Having thought that you were protected from rent increases (one of the main advantages of a lease), you won't take kindly to an increase mid-lease. But think carefully: It may be a mistake to point out to your landlord that the rent payment clause cannot be changed during the life of the lease. Especially if you have been habitually late paying rent or have broken some other significant provision for which you could be evicted (for example, your boyfriend has moved in, violating your lease's restrictions on occupants), you may end up winning the battle but losing the war. In short, if the landlord has a *legal* ground for eviction, it is probably far better to go along with the rent payment change than to stand on your rights and invite the end of your tenancy.

4. Rent Increases as Retaliation or Discrimination

Landlords may not raise the rent in a discriminatory manner—for example, only for members of a certain race or religion or for families with children. (Discrimination is explained in detail in Chapter 5.)

Also, in most states your landlord can't use a rent increase (or evict you or decrease services, either) in retaliation against you for exercising a specified legal right. For example, if you make a legitimate complaint to a public agency about defective conditions in your rental unit, your landlord may not raise your rent to punish you. (Chapter 7 discusses your rights to demand fit and habitable housing, and Chapter 11 explains what you can do about landlord retaliation.)

5. Talking the Landlord out of a Rent Increase

Legally, there is nothing you can do about a legal rent hike that doesn't violate a rent control ordinance and is not discriminatory or retaliatory. The landlord can charge as much as the market will bear. But, practically, you can appeal to your landlord's business sense.

Landlording is a business with the goal of making money, but smart landlords realize that high rents are not the only route to high profits. Solvent, long-term tenants are the best tenants because they are low-maintenance—they don't have to be evicted, sued, coddled, cleaned up after, scolded for breaking the rules, or interviewed and investigated as part of the time- and money-consuming new-tenant application process. If you are a good, long-term tenant and can convince your landlord that the rent hike will make you move, your landlord might think twice, or at least moderate the increase. (On the other hand, if you have been less than straight in your dealings with the landlord, don't expect any accommodations.)

 When faced with a rent hike, work together with other long-term tenants. Your leverage with the landlord will increase if you can show that many other stable, long-term tenants are also upset and considering moving. If the rent hike affects others in your building, work together to present your collective plea. Remember, even in a tight rental market, lots of long-term tenants are hard to find.

H. The Landlord's Right to Change Other Rent Terms

If you've bounced a check or two or lost your job, can your landlord suddenly refuse personal checks and accept only certified checks or money orders? Or, if you've been paying by mail, can your landlord now require you to bring your rent to the manager's office?

Legally, the answer to these questions is usually no—assuming your payment method has followed the instructions on this issue in your lease or rental agreement. If you have a year's lease, the payment arrangement is in force for a year; if you rent month to month, most states require your landlord to give at least 30 days' written notice before changing a rental agreement clause.

If your lease or rental agreement doesn't say where and how rent is to be paid, your landlord's past practice is likely to legally control how rent is paid. For example, a landlord who has always asked for your rent check on the first of the month has established a due date that both of you must honor until the landlord formally changes the system with proper notice (in most states, 30 days).

RULES TO RENT BY

- **Always pay rent on time.** Do whatever it takes, including hand-delivering your rent check. If you mail your rent check, make sure that it arrives on time—it is not sufficient to post your check on the rent due date.
- **If you can't pay on time, deal with it.** Contact the landlord, explain the situation and offer a partial payment and a plan to pay the rest. If he agrees, send a letter of understanding (see Chapter 2, Section G) that will protect you in case your landlord "forgets" and attempts to terminate for nonpayment of rent.
- **Think carefully before refusing to pay late fees.** Although they may be illegal, it may not be worth risking an eviction lawsuit to prove your point.

Chapter 4

Security Deposits

Most landlords will require a security deposit before you move in. If you damage the property or leave owing rent, your landlord can use your deposit to cover what you owe. Deposits can amount to several hundreds, or even thousands of dollars and are a major source of friction between landlords and tenants as to the amount charged, whether or not it's refundable, and how it's used.

Fortunately, many states impose fairly strict rules on how landlords can collect and use deposits and how they must return them when tenants move out. Some states and cities even require landlords to put deposits in a separate account and pay interest on them. Landlords who violate security deposit laws are often subject to substantial financial penalties. (Appendix 2 provides details on state security deposit rules, including limits, whether the landlord must keep your money in a separate account or pay you interest on it, and the deadline for returning the deposit after you leave.)

If you live in an area that regulates security deposits, count yourself lucky. If you don't, it's especially important that you follow our advice on clarifying the use and return of all deposits with your landlord *before* you move in. To protect yourself and avoid the all-too-common misunderstandings with your landlord, make sure your lease or rental agreement clearly states:

- what you must do to ensure the return of your deposit, and
- how soon after you vacate the unit your landlord will assess the condition of your rental and return all or part of the deposit.

If the game plan isn't contained in your rental documents, you can always ask the landlord for his requirements and procedures and then write a letter of understanding documenting what he said. (Letters of understanding are explained in Chapter 2, Section G.)

A. Dollar Limits on Security Deposits

Half the states don't set any limits on deposits. As with rent, landlords are free to charge as much deposit as they want. But unless the rental market is especially tight, landlords won't find many takers if they charge a security deposit of more than a month or two of rent.

The other half of the states limit the deposit a landlord can collect to an amount equal to one or two months of rent. The deposit limit that applies to you may depend on factors such as:

- your age (senior citizens may have a lower deposit ceiling)
- whether or not the rental unit is furnished (sometimes larger deposits are allowed for furnished apartments)
- whether or not you have a pet or waterbed (if so, you'll often pay a higher deposit), and
- the number of rental properties the landlord owns (smaller landlords may be exempt from security deposit limits).

(Check "State Security Deposit Laws" in Appendix 2 to see whether your state limits the amount your landlord can collect.)

Negotiate the amount and payment of deposits. If you have a hard time coming up with the deposit, your landlord may allow you to pay the deposit in installments or may actually reduce it. Here are a few tips for approaching your landlord. Obviously, these strategies are more likely to work if you have a good credit history and references and live in an area with lots of rentals. And don't ask for a lower deposit or an installment plan until you know for sure the place is yours.

- Offer to pay half the deposit up front with the rest on an affordable installment plan. Some landlords will say yes only if you can come up with the whole deposit in 30 to 60 days, but others will let you increase the amount a little each month until it's topped off in six months or more.

- Offer to pay higher rent in exchange for a substantially lower deposit. For example, offer to pay $25 more per month for the first year in exchange for the landlord cutting the security deposit from $1,000 to $500. Even though the landlord would only get an extra $300 in one year while you get a break of $500, the landlord knows that the $300 is his to keep, unlike money paid as a refundable deposit.

B. How Landlords May Increase Deposits

If you have a fixed-term lease, your landlord may not raise the security deposit during the term of your lease, unless the lease itself allows it (most don't). If you have a month-to-month tenancy, a security deposit can be increased just the same way the rent can be, typically by giving you a written notice 30 days in advance of the change. (See Chapter 3, Section G.) Of course, if your state regulates the maximum deposit that can be charged, your landlord can't exceed that amount.

C. What's the Money For?

By law in most states, your landlord must refund your deposit promptly after you move out, unless there is a valid reason not to return all or part of it. Most states give landlords a set amount of time (usually from 14 to 30 days) to either return your entire deposit or provide an itemized written statement of deductions and refund the rest.

Although state laws vary on the details, your landlord can almost always withhold all or part of the deposit to pay for:

- unpaid rent
- repairing damage to the premises (except for "ordinary wear and tear") that you or a guest caused

- cleaning necessary to restore the rental unit to its condition at the beginning of the tenancy (over and above "ordinary wear and tear"), and

- replacing rental unit property you've taken.

Landlords don't need to wait until you move out to tap into your security deposit. Your landlord may use some of it during your tenancy—for example, because you broke or damaged something and didn't fix or pay for it. After using part of the deposit in this way, the landlord may require you to replenish it. (Chapter 10 explains how landlords may use the deposit when you move out.)

D. Last Month's Rent

A landlord may want you to pay a sum of money called "last month's rent" before you move in as a form of insurance against your leaving without giving the proper amount of notice. If you've paid for the last month in a payment clearly labeled "last month's rent," you obviously don't have to pay for the last month.

Many states consider a last month's rent payment as part of the security deposit when it comes to limits. In other words, if your state limits security deposits to twice the monthly rent, your landlord can collect for the last month and only one more monthly sum as "security." But he can't collect twice the monthly rent as a deposit *plus* the last month's rent.

USING THE SECURITY DEPOSIT AS THE LAST MONTH'S RENT

Many tenants are tempted not to pay their last month's rent, figuring that the landlord will just take it out of their deposit. This is a risky move.

- Forcing the landlord to deplete the deposit to cover rent leaves him with less money to use should he need to make repairs or replace missing items in your unit. Even if you leave the place spotless, your landlord won't appreciate being manipulated this way. Don't expect a good reference when your next landlord asks about you as a tenant.

- Even though you've announced that you're leaving, your landlord may still send you a termination notice and follow-up with an eviction lawsuit. He may simply not trust you to leave, and may not want to waste any time getting you out once your rent payments have stopped. Even if the eviction is dismissed, you'll have it on your credit record, which will be a major problem for future rentals.

- Laws in a few states, including Kansas, Minnesota, and Texas, impose penalties on tenants who attempt to use the deposit as the last month's rent without their landlord's permission.

If you want to use the deposit for the last month's rent, ask the landlord and get his okay in writing.

E. Nonrefundable Deposits and Fees

Many landlords collect a fee that is not refundable—such as for pets or cleaning. A few states such as California specifically prohibit landlords from charging any fee or deposit that is not refundable, but most state security deposit statutes are silent on the subject of nonrefundable fees or allow them for specific purposes such as cleaning.

If you're being charged a nonrefundable fee, check your state security deposit laws (citations are in Appendix 2) to see whether your state regulates this practice. Even if nonrefundable fees are allowed, be sure you're clear on what the fee covers.

F. Are You Entitled to Interest on Your Deposit?

Unfair as it may seem, only a third of the states require landlords to pay interest on deposits. In other words, many landlords can simply put your deposit in a personal bank account, use it, and pocket the interest, as long as the original sum is available when you move out.

Some states require landlords to give tenants information on the location of this separate trust account at the start of the tenancy, usually as part of the lease or rental agreement. These states typically establish detailed requirements, including:

- **The interest rate to be paid.** Usually, it's a little lower than the bank actually pays because the landlord is allowed to keep a small portion for administrative expenses.
- **When interest payments must be made.** The most common laws require payments to be made annually and/or when you leave.
- **Notifying the tenant.** Landlords must tell tenants where and how the security deposit is being held and the rate of interest it's earning.

Chicago, Los Angeles, San Francisco, and several other cities (typically those with rent control) require landlords to pay or credit tenants with interest on security deposits even if the state law does not impose this duty. A few cities require that the funds be kept in interest-bearing accounts that are separate from the landlord's personal or other business accounts.

Ask for interest. Excellent landlords are willing to pay interest on your deposit as an honest business practice, even if there is no law requiring it. If your landlord doesn't volunteer to do this, there's no harm in asking.

G. How Your Landlord's Bankruptcy or Property Sale Affects Your Deposit

If your building has been sold or the landlord has gone belly-up and declared bankruptcy, your security deposit should still be available to you (minus legitimate deductions for damage or unpaid rent) at the end of your tenancy. That's the theory, at any rate. You may still have to take steps to retrieve your deposit.

1. When the Landlord Declares Bankruptcy

If your landlord files for bankruptcy, your security deposit is beyond the reach of his creditors. That's because, technically speaking, it's not your landlord's money—it's yours, which must be returned to you unless you fail to pay the rent or damage the property. Of course, if the landlord has used up every bit of cash within reach, there simply may not be any funds immediately available to pay you.

Don't give up, however, if your landlord pleads poverty and shrugs. Remember, declaring bankruptcy doesn't mean that she gets to walk away from her debts and keep inessential frills. The court will appoint a bankruptcy trustee who will assemble the creditors and pay them with what's left of the landlord's assets. Sometimes nonliquid assets (cars, real property, or jewelry) are sold to make funds available. Since you are not even a creditor, you should be at or near the top of the list. Contact the bankruptcy court (listed in the government pages of your phone book under "United States Courts") and write to the trustee, explaining your situation and asking to be paid.

2. If the Building Is Sold

In most states, the law requires a landlord who sells the building to do one of two things: Return the deposit to the tenant or transfer it to the new owner. If the old owner simply walks off with the deposit, the new owner cannot require you to pay again. He'll have to come up with the money when it's time to return the deposit to you. If he refuses, you'll have to sue him, preferably in small claims court. (See Chapter 13.) In some states, you can also sue the former owner.

RULES TO RENT BY

The security deposit demanded by your landlord is likely to be a hefty chunk of change. Take steps to ensure that you get it back:

- **Know the law.** Check to see whether your state sets a maximum security deposit. If you're being asked to pay a nonrefundable fee, find out whether it's legal and, if so, if it counts towards your state's limit, if any.
- **Learn the landlord's rules.** Find out at the beginning what steps you must take to get the security deposit back. For example, does your landlord's definition of "clean" include waxing the linoleum floors, or simply mopping them?
- **Don't assume that the deposit will cover the last month's rent unless the landlord agrees.** In some states, this dodge will cost you plenty because it will allow the landlord to keep some of the remaining deposit that you otherwise would get back. And, in all states, you can count on a negative reference from this landlord when a prospective landlord calls for a read on you.

Chapter 5

Discrimination

Not so long ago, a landlord could refuse to rent to you or evict you for almost any reason—because of your skin color, or your religion, or because you had children or were elderly or disabled. Some landlords even discriminated against single women, believing that they would be incapable of paying the rent or would have too many overnight guests.

Recognizing that all Americans who could afford to pay the rent should have the right to live where they chose, Congress and state legislatures passed laws prohibiting housing discrimination. Most notable of these are the federal Fair Housing Act of 1968 and the federal Fair Housing Amendments Act of 1988, which outlaw discrimination based on race or color, national origin, religion, sex, familial status, or disability. These laws are administered by the Department of Housing and Urban Development (HUD). In addition, many states and cities have laws making it illegal to discriminate based on additional factors, such as marital status or sexual orientation.

Today, it is safe to say that unless a landlord has a legitimate business reason to reject a prospective tenant (for example, a poor credit history or terrible references from previous landlords), she risks a potentially costly legal challenge.

In this chapter, we'll explain the federal antidiscrimination protections that apply to every tenant and alert you to some state protections as well. And we'll suggest what you can do if you feel that you have been the victim of illegal discrimination.

A. Discrimination Prohibited by Federal Laws

Since federal law governs everyone, we'll start with it. A number of federal laws prohibit discrimination on the basis of the following criteria (called "protected categories"):

- race or color
- religion
- national origin
- familial status or age—includes families with children under the age of 18 and pregnant women
- disability or handicap, or
- sex.

The federal Fair Housing Acts apply to all aspects of the landlord-tenant relationship. A landlord may not:

- advertise or make any statement that indicates a limitation or preference based on race, religion, or any other protected category
- falsely deny that a rental unit is available
- set more restrictive standards for selecting tenants or refuse to rent to members of certain groups
- before or during the tenancy, set different terms, conditions, or privileges for rental of a dwelling unit, such as requiring larger deposits of some tenants or adopting an inconsistent policy of responding to late rent payments
- terminate a tenancy for a discriminatory reason.

FEDERAL LOOPHOLES, STATE PLUGS

Unfortunately, not every rental is covered by the federal fair housing laws. The following types of property are exempt:

- owner-occupied buildings with four or fewer rental units
- single-family housing rented without the use of advertising or without a real estate broker, as long as the landlord owns no more than three such homes at any one time
- certain types of housing operated by religious organizations and private clubs that limit occupancy to their own members, and
- with respect to age discrimination only, housing reserved exclusively for senior citizens. There are two kinds of senior citizen housing exempted: communities where every tenant is 62 years of age or older, or "55 and older" communities in which at least 80% of the occupied units must be occupied by at least one person 55 years or older.

Fortunately for some tenants, however, many states step in with their own laws to cover properties or situations that are exempt under federal law. For example, owner-occupied buildings with four or fewer rental units are exempt under federal law but are protected under California law.

---

1. Race or Religion

Overt discrimination against persons of a certain race or religion ("No blacks allowed") is unusual but, incredibly, does still occur. Far more common is subtle discrimination that is accomplished by indirect methods. For example, the landlord who turns away every black applicant is discriminating just as much as the one who announces that none need apply. And an apartment ad that says "safe Christian community" or "Sunday quiet times enforced" violates federal law, since applicants might reasonably conclude that Christians are preferred as tenants.

2. National Origin

Discrimination based on national origin is illegal, whether it's deliberate or carried out indirectly. For instance, an ad that offers special discounts to members of the Italian-American Club would be a likely candidate for a discrimination charge. And landlords cannot require proof of citizenship or immigration papers from applicants of one ethnicity but not from others, since doing so places a burden on one group that is not imposed on everyone else.

3. Familial Status or Age

Landlords are not allowed to explicitly or indirectly turn you away based on your family status or your age.

a. Discrimination Against Families

While some landlords don't like renting to tenants with children, fearing the noise and wear and tear that kids might cause, the federal Fair Housing Acts prohibit discriminating on this basis. A landlord may not legally turn away or evict a tenant because he or she has children or because an applicant or tenant is pregnant. Even if the landlord has a worthy motive, such as believing that children won't be safe in the building or the neighborhood, he is not permitted to deny the tenancy on that basis or to make other discriminatory moves such as steering families to certain parts of the property (usually the back).

Some landlords try to get around the laws prohibiting discrimination against families by setting unreasonably low occupancy limits, such as only two people for a two-bedroom unit. This too is illegal, as it would have the effect of excluding families. Federal law (in this case, an opinion letter written by the Department of Housing and Urban Development) has established minimum occupancy standards that regulate how low an occupancy can go and still be legal. In general, landlords must allow at least two persons per bedroom. Landlords can be more restrictive only in rare instances, when they can show that legitimate business reasons justify a harsher standard. For example, a policy of only three persons in a two-bedroom unit might pass muster if the landlord can prove it is truly based on the limitations of the plumbing system or some other aspect of the building's infrastructure.

Some states are more generous to tenants (by law, states cannot reduce the protections offered by federal law). For example, because California state law allows two occupants per bedroom plus one more occupant in the whole unit, a California landlord renting a three-bedroom apartment must allow seven occupants, unless she can point to legitimate business reasons justifying a lower number. Finally, some local governments have also written occupancy laws—but they, too, are legal only if they are more generous to the tenant than the federal standard or any state law.

b. Age Discrimination

The federal Fair Housing Acts do not expressly ban discrimination based on age. Nevertheless, it is definitely forbidden under the broader prohibition against discrimination on the basis of familial status.

A landlord cannot refuse to rent to an older person or impose special terms and conditions on the tenancy unless these same standards are applied to everyone else. If you have excellent references and credit history, a landlord has no legal basis for refusing you, even if you are 95 and rely to some degree on the regular assistance of a nearby adult child or friend. (Of course, a landlord could legally give the rental to someone else with equal or better references or financial stability.) However, if your current landlord reveals that you suffer from advanced senility to the point that you often wander into the wrong apartment, frequently forget to pay the rent, or are unable to undertake basic housekeeping chores, the prospective landlord can refuse to rent to you based on this age-neutral evidence that you are not likely to be a stable, reliable tenant.

4. Disability

Federal law prohibits discrimination against people who:

- have a physical or mental disability that substantially limits one or more major life activities—including, but not limited to, hearing, mobility and visual impairments; chronic alcoholism (but only if it is being addressed through a recovery program); mental illness; mental retardation; being HIV-positive, having AIDS or AIDS-Related Complex
- have a history or record of such a disability, or
- are regarded by others to have such a disability.

a. Mental or Emotional Impairments

If you had, have, or appear to have mental or emotional impairments, you must be evaluated and treated by the landlord on the basis of your financial stability and history as a tenant, not on the basis of your mental health. If you cannot meet the good-tenant criteria that the landlord applies to all applicants (such as a minimum rent-to-income ratio), you may be rejected on that basis.

b. Discriminatory Questions and Actions

Landlords are not allowed to ask you whether or not you have a disability or illness or ask to see medical records. And no matter how well intentioned, the landlord cannot make decisions about where and how you will live on the property that he would not make were you not disabled. For example, if there are two units for rent—one on the ground floor and one three stories up—the landlord must show both units to a wheelchair-bound applicant unless the applicant asks to see only one.

c. The Rights of Disabled Tenants to Live in an Accessible Place

Federal law protects disabled tenants after they have moved into a rental unit as well as during the application process. Landlords must reasonably accommodate the needs of disabled tenants, at the landlord's own expense. This means that a disabled tenant should expect her landlord to adjust rules, procedures, or services to a reasonable degree in order to give her an equal opportunity to use and enjoy her dwelling unit or a common space. Examples include the provision of a parking space for a movement-impaired tenant and the acceptance of a guide or service animal in an otherwise "no pets" building.

However, landlords need not undertake changes that would seriously impair their ability to run their business, such as installing an elevator to the third floor to accommodate a wheelchair-bound tenant's wish to live there.

Fortunately, where a landlord's legal duty to reasonably accommodate the needs of a disabled tenant ends, his obligation to allow the tenant to modify the living space may begin. A disabled tenant has the right to modify his living space, at the tenant's expense, to the extent necessary to make the space safe and comfortable. There are two caveats to this rule: First, the landlord is not required to allow you to make major structural alterations. Second, if the modifications will make the unit unacceptable to the next tenant, the disabled tenant must agree to undo the modification when moving out. The landlord has the right to insist that the tenant put money in an escrow account to cover the eventual cost of returning the unit to its original condition. Examples of modifications undertaken by a disabled tenant include the lowering of countertops, installation of a ramp, or repositioning the light switches.

Landlords are entitled to ask for proof that the accommodation or modification you have requested will address your situation—without it, your landlord has no way of knowing whether your request is legitimate or a ruse to obtain special treatment. Ask your physician or therapist for a letter attesting that what you are asking for will meet your needs. To protect your privacy, explain to the physician or other writer that he need not explain the disability. He need only certify that you are under his care and that the changes you would like are appropriate to your situation.

LIMITED PROTECTION FOR ALCOHOLICS AND DRUG USERS

Federal fair housing law extends limited protection to two carefully defined groups:

- recovering alcoholics—those who actively and regularly participate in a medically based treatment or AA program
- former drug addicts—including those who have prior convictions for illegal drug use (but not for drug dealing or manufacture).

It is important to remember that, despite these protections, other aspects of a recovering alcoholic's (or a former drug addict's) past might legally serve as the basis for a denial of housing. For example, if you are a recovering alcoholic who has bad credit, a spotty employment history, or negative references from your previous landlords, a landlord may reject you for these reasons just as readily as any other applicant with these flaws. What a landlord cannot do is reject a prospective tenant solely on the basis of his status as a former addict or recovering alcoholic.

---

5. Sex and Sexual Harassment

You cannot be denied a place to live (or have special rules imposed on you) solely because you're female or male. Even well-intentioned policies are off-limits—for example, fearful that single women are more likely to be burglarized and assaulted than male tenants, a landlord cannot require single females to live in upper-story apartments, even if, in fact, those units are less prone to break-ins.

Sexual harassment is another form of unlawful sexual discrimination. For example, it's illegal to refuse to rent to a person who resists the landlord's sexual advances or to make life difficult for a tenant who has resisted such advances.

B. Kinds of Discrimination Prohibited by State and Local Law

Most state and local laws prohibiting housing discrimination echo federal antidiscrimination law. But some laws forbid additional types of discrimination—such as discrimination based on marital status— that aren't covered by federal law. For example, in states that prohibit discrimination based on marital status, it would be illegal to refuse to rent to divorced people, even though federal law does not prohibit this kind of discrimination.

Here we explain some of the common antidiscrimination laws that states and localities have adopted. For more information on state and local housing discrimination laws, contact your state fair housing agency.

1. Marital Status

About 20 states ban discrimination on the basis of marital status. Most of these states' laws extend protection to married couples only (meaning that landlords cannot treat them differently from single tenants). Oddly, courts in Maryland, Minnesota, New York, and Wisconsin, where marital discrimination is also recognized, extend the protection only to *single* renters (landlords cannot treat them differently from married tenants).

What about unmarried couples? In most states, landlords may legally refuse to rent to you if you are an unmarried couple. This means that landlords in these states may legally ask if two applicants of the same or different sex are lovers or just friendly roommates. In Alaska, California,

Massachusetts, Michigan, and New Jersey, however, courts have ruled that the term "marital status" extends to unmarried couples. In these states, landlords cannot refuse to rent to you simply because you and your roommate are not married.

2. Sexual Orientation

Housing discrimination based on sexual orientation is prohibited in California, Connecticut, the District of Columbia, Massachusetts, Minnesota, New Jersey, Rhode Island, Vermont, and Wisconsin. In addition, many cities prohibit discrimination against gays and lesbians, including Atlanta, Chicago, Detroit, Miami, New York, Pittsburgh, St. Louis, and Seattle. For more information on state or local law on sexual orientation, contact the National Gay & Lesbian Task Force, 1700 Kalorama Road NW, Washington, DC 20009; 202-332-6483; or check out their website at www.ngltf.org.

If you or your roommate are gay or lesbian and you live in a state or city that extends antidiscrimination protection to you, a landlord may not ask for details of your intimate lives.

3. Source of Income

In a few states, including, Minnesota, New Jersey, and North Dakota, applicants who receive public assistance may not be turned away or otherwise discriminated against solely because of this fact. But a landlord may refuse to rent to you if your available income—regardless of its source—falls below a reasonable level, as long as the same standard is applied to every applicant. And landlords in most states (though not in Connecticut or New Jersey) are not required to participate in the federal housing subsidy program known as Section 8.

C. How to Fight Back

If you believe that a landlord has unlawfully discriminated against you, you can try to work things out with the landlord, or you can take advantage of the powerful antidiscrimination laws discussed earlier.

Your options (discussed below) include:

- trying to negotiate an acceptable settlement with the landlord, possibly with the help of a neutral mediator
- filing a complaint with a federal, state, or local government fair housing agency, or
- filing a lawsuit in federal or state court.

If successful, these strategies may force the landlord to do one or more of the following:

- Rent you a particular unit.
- Pay you "actual" or "compensatory" damages, which cover what you spent to find another rental, such as money spent on another apartment-finding service or taking several hours off from your job. These damages also cover any additional rent you had to pay elsewhere. In addition, you are entitled to be compensated for any humiliation or emotional distress (called "special damages") that you suffered due to the landlord's bad acts. If the landlord's conduct was truly awful, this amount can be substantial.
- Pay you punitive damages, which essentially punishes the land-lord for especially outrageous, intentional discrimination.
- Pay your attorney fees and court costs, if any.
- Pay a penalty to the government.

1. What Do You Want to Accomplish?

Before you can make an intelligent decision about what strategy to pursue, you need to sit down and ask yourself what you're trying to achieve.

Quick results. If you simply want the offensive or unfair behavior to stop, and aren't interested in seeking compensation for your expenses, inconvenience, or humiliation, it doesn't make sense to file a complaint or lawsuit right away. A frank discussion with the landlord, perhaps in the company of a mediator or other neutral third party, may work better than a full-frontal legal assault. (Chapter 13 gives advice on how to negotiate with your landlord. If informal techniques don't work, you still can sue or complain to a government agency.)

Major changes. If negotiation hasn't worked, or if you feel that compensation is necessary, a lawsuit may be the necessary course of action. But be forewarned: Lawsuits and complaints to fair housing agencies are adversarial, miserable, drawn-out procedures. And keep in mind that even if you win, the fact that you filed a discrimination complaint may appear on your credit record for some years into the future—not an endearing bit of information to your next landlord's eyes. If a prospective landlord or employer asks the credit bureau to run an "investigative consumer report" (containing detailed information about your character, general reputation, personal characteristics, and mode of living), you can be sure that this episode will show up. (Credit reports are covered in Chapter 1, Section B.)

Before making a final decision as to which path to take, ask for the opinion of a trusted and reasonable friend. Discrimination can be a highly emotional subject, and it's always a good idea to seek the counsel of someone who is not involved.

Don't proceed alone. If the landlord's insurance company or lawyer realizes you have complained to a fair housing agency (or are about to do so) or are poised to file a lawsuit, they may offer to settle. Be wary of dealing with insurance or legal professionals without the presence of a neutral third party such as a mediator. (Chapter 13, Section B, explains the mediation process and gives you information on locating and working with a mediator.)

Mediate, Don't Litigate, by Peter Lovenheim and Lisa Guerin (Nolo), contains important information on choosing and working with a mediator.

HOW STRONG IS YOUR CASE?

If you've decided you want to file a complaint with a fair housing agency or to sue the landlord, you need to evaluate the strength of your case. The following guidelines will help you judge how strong or weak a case you have.

- **The more serious the harm you suffered, the more likely you are to win.** Be realistic in your assessment: A muttered racial slur will not offend a judge as much as a landlord's flat-out statement that he will not rent to you because you're Jewish or black.
- **Repeated acts of discrimination are more likely to earn the wrath of a judge than a single incident.** If you can point to a pattern of illegal discrimination rather than an isolated incident, you're way ahead. And don't forget that judges have long memories—your landlord may be well known in the local HUD office for his behavior, which will make your case all the more plausible.
- **Although unintentional discrimination is as illegal as intentional acts, it is harder to prove.** For example, although an occupancy policy of "one person per bedroom" has the effect of discriminating against families, it's harder to prove this than if the landlord had a stated policy of "no children."
- **If you have only your word against the landlord's, you have a weak case.** As with any lawsuit, you need independent, physical evidence of your claims—like witnesses who will testify, newspaper ads, or house rules that establish the discriminatory policy—to corroborate your word.

2. Complaining to a Fair Housing Agency

You may file a discrimination complaint with the federal department of Housing and Urban Development (HUD) if you believe a federal law has been violated. Similarly, you can file with a state antidiscrimination agency if your state's antidiscrimination law has been violated. Some areas also have local fair housing agencies that handle complaints.

A complaint to HUD must be filed within one year of the alleged violation. HUD will investigate the allegation and, if it concludes that there is a basis for your claim, will attempt a conciliation (compromise) between you and the landlord. If a compromise isn't reached, HUD will bring the case before an administrative law judge who, without a jury, will decide the matter and may award you money damages or order the landlord to take appropriate action. State and local laws may have different procedures, including shorter filing deadlines, than those used by HUD.

3. Filing a Lawsuit in Federal or State Court

If you have experienced clear and outrageous discrimination, going directly to court may be quicker and more rewarding than going to a government agency. You'll need the help of an experienced lawyer if you choose this route. If you file in federal court, you must do so within two years of the alleged violation.

Your lawyer may ask the court for an immediate order, called a temporary restraining order or a preliminary injunction, that orders the landlord to do (or not to do) something (such as offer you the rental or cease treating you in a negative way) pending a full trial. Often, cases settle after an order like this is made.

You'll need to understand how lawyers typically charge for these types of cases. You may be asked to pay an up-front amount called a retainer, or the lawyer may take the case "on contingency," which means that she'll take a certain percent (usually 20% to 40%) if you win.

RULES TO RENT BY

- **Remember that landlords are allowed to discriminate for legitimate business reasons** such as whether you smoke or have pets, but not on other grounds that are prohibited by federal or state law.
- **Federal law prohibits discrimination on the basis of race or color, religion, national origin, familial status, age, disability, or sex.** State and local laws sometimes offer additional protections, such as prohibiting discrimination on the basis of marital status or sexual orientation.
- **Discrimination takes several forms.** It may be explicit ("No children allowed") or subtle ("A quiet, adult community"). Either way, if the effect is to discriminate against a protected group, it is illegal.
- **If you feel that you've been discriminated against,** before marching into the nearest lawyers' suite, sit down with a friend who can give you straight advice. Ask yourself: What do I want to accomplish? Do I have a realistic appraisal of the harm I've suffered, and do I have solid evidence to back it up? Am I willing to become entangled in a lawsuit? Formulate your strategy accordingly.

MORE INFORMATION ON DISCRIMINATION

The law. The federal antidiscrimination laws, known as the Fair Housing Act of 1968 and the Fair Housing Amendments Act of 1988, are in a set of code books called the United States Code and can be found at 42 United States Code Sections 3601–3619 and 3631. On the Web, you can read the law by going to Nolo's website (www. nolo.com) and (midway down the page) using our Free Information and Tools. Choose the U.S. Laws and Regulations link in the Legal Research Center, then type in the volume and section number of the part of the code you'd like to read.

Where to complain. Regional HUD offices can be reached by calling HUD's Fair Housing Information Clearinghouse at 800-343-3442. They are also listed on the HUD website: www.hud.gov. Your state's fair housing agency and state consumer protection office are listed on the site maintained by the Federal Consumer Information Center at http://consumeraction.gov/state.shtm .

Chapter 6

Roommates

If you're like most tenants, you've got one roommate or more. And chances are that the names on your mailbox will change at least once before you, too, move on. Unfortunately, many landlords aren't as flexible as you would like when it comes to adding new roommates or letting others out of a lease.

This chapter discusses key aspects of sharing your home, including:

- your legal obligations and responsibilities with respect to your roommates
- what to do if your roommate takes off, leaving you with the rent to pay and maybe damages to cover
- moving in a roommate and what to do if your landlord objects
- what to do if your roommate becomes nasty or won't pay the rent, and
- whether or not you can rent space to a roomer.

LEGAL JARGON YOU NEED TO KNOW

Try as we might, we couldn't completely eliminate the legal buzz words in this chapter. You need to understand them, because your rights and responsibilities will vary depending on the term that fits your situation. For example, tenants can make some demands on their landlords that subtenants cannot, as explained below. Here's a list of the essential ones, with nutshell definitions.

Original tenant. The initial tenant (or tenants) who entered into the lease or rental agreement (oral or written). This is our own short-cut term with no precise legal meaning.

Tenant. Someone who has signed a lease or a rental agreement, or was part of an oral rental agreement, or whose residency has otherwise been accepted by the landlord (by accepting rent, for example). Since he has a direct relationship with the landlord, a tenant can hold the landlord to all the landlord's promises (in the lease or rental agreement).

Cotenants. Two or more tenants who rent the same property under the same lease or rental agreement. Each is 100% responsible for carrying out the agreement (see "joint and several liability," below), including paying the rent in full. Someone who is added to another's lease or rental agreement becomes the original tenant's (or tenants') cotenant.

Subtenant. Someone who rents from a tenant. The tenant becomes the subtenant's landlord. The subtenant may take over for a portion of the lease term (for the summer, for example, with the tenant returning in September), or may live there at the same time as the tenant. Subtenants have an indirect relationship with the main landlord, and therefore cannot enforce many of the lease or rental agreement terms. Throughout this book, when we speak of "tenants," we do not mean subtenants unless specifically noted.

Roommates. Two or more people living under the same roof and sharing rent and expenses. Roommates are usually cotenants (they've signed the same lease or rental agreement), but a roommate may instead be a subtenant of the original tenant. Unless the landlord has accepted the presence of the roommate (by making her a cotenant or explicitly or tacitly allowing the subtenancy), a roommate has the legal status of a long-term guest, with few if any legal protections.

Joint and several liability. This refers to the sharing of legal obligations by two or more people. Cotenants are "jointly and severally liable" for rent and other obligations of the lease, which means that each one can be held responsible for the misdeeds of the others and the landlord can look to any one of them to pay the entire rent. This is true even if your lease or rental agreement does not include this clause. It applies to oral leases, too.

Roomer. A person who rents space in your home while you live there. If you are a tenant, the roomer (sometimes called "lodger") is your subtenant, and you are her landlord. In most situations, landlords may legally prohibit roomers.

A. Renting a Place With Others

When two or more people sign the same rental agreement or lease—or enter into the same oral rental agreement—they are cotenants and share the same legal rights and responsibilities. But there's a special twist, which you may have noticed when reading "Legal Jargon," above. The legal principle known as "joint and several liability" has enormous implications for cotenants. You could snooze through the rest of this chapter and still come out okay if you pay attention to this one important point.

Keep in mind that here we are talking about housemates who are *cotenants*, not tenant and subtenant. This is an important distinction. A tenant and his subtenant do not share the same rights and responsibilities with respect to each other or to the landlord. If you are a tenant who has rented out part of your place to someone else, or who has allowed someone to live there instead of you for a portion of time, you are dealing with a subtenancy. Skip ahead to Section D, below, in which we explain the legal landscape of tenants and subtenants.

1. Joint and Several Liability: You're in This Together

Joint and several liability is the legal version of the slogan of the Three Musketeers: "One for all and all for one." Here's what it means to tenants:

- **One for all.** The landlord can demand the entire rent from just one cotenant. The rent-sharing understanding you have with your roommates is immaterial to the landlord. In other words, even if you pay $100 for your tiny room and your roommate pays $500 for a master suite, you'll be liable for the full $600 rent if for some reason your roommate flakes out.

- **All for one.** Even innocent cotenants will suffer the conse-quences of one cotenant's misdeeds. Unfair as it seems, the raucous party that your roommate threw when you were out of town can result in a termination notice directed to you, too.

It's that simple. So how can you avoid being tarred by your room-mate's screw-ups? The best answer, of course, is to choose your house-mates carefully. Even solid friendships will benefit from thinking ahead to possible areas of friction and planning ways to avoid problems.

⚠️ **Only landlords can evict tenants.** This means that cotenants cannot force each other out. If your roommate becomes insufferable, you'll have to work it out between the two of you unless his behavior is *also* a violation of a lease or rental agreement clause (for example, illegal drug use). Although a violation of this nature would justify the termination of *both* your tenancies (joint and several liability!), you might get lucky if your landlord pities you and lets you stay.

2. Talk It Out and Write It Down

Roommates make lots of informal agreements about splitting rent, sharing chores, and choosing bedrooms. It's important to understand that such agreements do not affect the joint and several liability of cotenants to the landlord, as discussed above. Just because you and your cotenants agreed to share cleaning and maintenance duties doesn't change the fact that each one of you is liable for any damage done to the apartment. And just as your landlord isn't bound by any agreements between roommates, your landlord cannot enforce them, either. If one roommate breaks an agreement she made with the rest of her cotenants to pay one-third the rent, don't bother asking your landlord to force her to pay up.

Since the arrangements between you and your roommates will have a huge effect on your day-to-day life, you should take them seriously. Before you move in, sit down with your roommates and discuss the major issues that are likely to come up, including:

- **Rent.** What is everyone's share? Who will write the rent check if the landlord will accept only one check?
- **Space.** Who will occupy which bedrooms?
- **Household chores.** Who's responsible for cleaning, and on what schedule?
- **Food sharing.** Will you be sharing food? How about shopping and cooking responsibilities? How will you split the costs and work?
- **Noise.** When should stereos be turned off or down low?
- **Overnight guests.** Is it okay for boyfriends/girlfriends to stay over? How often?
- **Moving out.** If one of you decides to move, how much notice must be given to the rest of you? Must the departing tenant find an acceptable substitute?
- **Spats.** How will you handle disagreements among yourselves about your living arrangement? (Don't kid yourself—they will come up.) If you want a roommate to leave, how can it be done fairly?

It's best to put your understandings in writing and ask every roommate to sign it. Oral agreements are too easily forgotten or misinterpreted after the fact. (See the Sample Roommate Agreement, below.)

A written and signed description of how you'll share the rent can help you collect if your roommate won't pay his share. Remember, if one roommate hasn't come up with his share, it's your problem—not the landlord's. You'll need to make up the deficit in order to avoid a termination. If your deadbeat roomie refuses to reimburse you, you can sue her in small claims court. A written and signed roommate understanding is important evidence in your favor.

SAMPLE ROOMMATE AGREEMENT

Catherine Davis, Kelli Halister, and Stacy Fremont are roommates at 3901 Bay, #123, Collegetown, CA, under a $900/month, year-long lease that begins on July 1, 2000, and expires on July 1, 2001. They have all signed the lease with the landlord, Will Skruoya; and have each paid $300 towards the security deposit of $900. Catherine, Kelli, and Stacy agree as follows:

1. Rent. Since Will has agreed to accept three separate checks; each will pay $300 on or before the first day of each month.

2. Food. Each roommate is responsible for her own food.

3. Cleaning. Each will clean her own room. Cleaning the bathroom and kitchen (appliances, counters, vacuuming, and mopping) and the living room (vacuuming and dusting) will be done once a week on a rotating basis.

---

4. Utilities. Everyone will pay an equal share of the electricity bill. Catherine will arrange for service, receive each monthly bill, and show it to the others within two days of receiving it. Kelli and Stacy will give Catherine their checks, made out to the electric company, within one day. Catherine will mail the payments.

5. Phone. Stacy will arrange for service, receive each monthly bill, and show it to the others within two days of receiving it. Within three days of receiving the bill, Catherine and Kelli will identify their long-distance and toll charges and give Stacy checks for them, plus one-third of the fixed charges, made out to the phone company. Stacy will mail the payments.

6. Guests. Each roommate agrees to have no more than one overnight guest at a time, except in extraordinary situations; and no more than four guests overnight in one month.

7. Parties. Each roommate agrees that there will be no social gatherings of more than three guests at which alcohol is served on school nights. Parties on Saturday or Sunday evenings will be reasonably managed by the hostess, who will clean up afterwards.

8. Exam Periods. During exams, no roommate will have overnight guests or parties.

9. Violations of This Agreement. The roommates agree that repeated and serious violations of this Agreement will be grounds for any two roommates to ask the other to leave. If a roommate is asked to leave, she will do so within one month and will forfeit any prepaid rent.

10. Leaving Before the Lease Ends. If a roommate wants to leave before the lease ends, she will give as much notice as possible (and not less than one month) and diligently try to find a replace-

ment tenant who is acceptable to the remaining roommates and the landlord.

11. Security Deposits. The roommate who leaves early (voluntarily or involuntarily) will get her share of the security deposit returned, minus rent, costs of repairs, replacement, and cleaning attributable to the departing tenant, when and if an acceptable new roommate signs the lease and contributes his/her share to the security deposit. If an acceptable replacement cannot be found, the departing roommate will not receive any portion of her share of the deposit until the tenancy of the remaining roommates is over and the deposit is refunded by the landlord.

12. Dispute Resolution. If a dispute arises concerning this Agreement or any aspect of the shared living situation, the roommates will ask the University Housing Office Mediation Service for assistance before they terminate the cotenancy or begin a lawsuit. This will involve all three roommates sitting down with the mediator in good faith to try to resolve the problems.

Catherine Davis	*June 15, 2000*
Catherine Davis	Date
Kelli Halister	*June 15, 2000*
Kelli Halister	Date
Stacy Fremont	*June 15, 2000*
Stacy Fremont	Date

GETTING RID OF A ROOMMATE

Despite your best efforts to choose compatible, considerate housemates, things may not work out as you planned. Maybe it's the roommate's personal habits or her failure to pay a fair share of expenses—whatever the rub, you may want her to leave. But if this roommate is a cotenant like you, you cannot legally force her out or ask the landlord to terminate her tenancy unless she has also broken one of the landlord's rules or engaged in illegal activity. So how can you convince her to move on? As is usually the case, the answer lies in preparation and negotiation.

Think ahead. If married couples can design prenuptial agreements, you can do the same for a roommate situation. At the start of your tenancy, before any tensions develop, design a fair way to deal with the problem. Paragraph 9 in our Sample Roommate Agreement, above, shows how three roommates decided they will deal with one who needs to go. If there are only two of you, you might agree that you'll go through mediation and abide by the mediator's suggestions (mediators usually don't impose decisions, but you can agree that you'll ask for one). The important point is to have a plan already in place that all have agreed to; that way, the problem roommate will be hard-pressed to opt out of the process.

Be creative. If you haven't planned ahead and are faced with an insufferable and stubborn roommate, you may need to use a little bribery. Paying someone to go is often very effective. And although most landlords won't get involved in their tenants' internal squabbles, you might try enlisting your landlord's help, anyway—the problem roomie may not know that the landlord cannot terminate her tenancy except for violations of the lease or of law, and a stern "Take off!" from the landlord might just do the trick.

B. When a Roommate Walks Out

All too frequently, living arrangements that look promising when you're just friends turn into disasters when you become housemates. Maybe it's the gym bag dumped on the kitchen table every evening, the inconsiderate parties on work nights, or the "occasional girlfriend" who turns out to be a regular, unpleasant presence. Getting a roommate to leave is difficult, as described in "Getting Rid of a Roommate," above. But what about the flip side—the consequences to those left behind when a roommate leaves suddenly or against the wishes of the others?

When cotenants split, there can be serious consequences beyond hurt feelings. The remaining roommates must scramble to cover the departed tenant's rent share, and the one who has moved on may find herself at the receiving end of a small claims court case demanding her share of rent. (Chapter 9 explains in detail the likely consequences to the departing tenant. Here we discuss the predicament of the remaining cotenants.)

First, some rules. In a month-to-month tenancy, a cotenant who wants to leave must give the landlord the required legal notice—30 days in most states. Forget trying to leave on short notice—most landlords won't prorate a month's rent. This means that the remaining tenants will have the same amount of time to hustle up a replacement. Of course, there is nothing wrong with cotenants deciding among themselves that they will give *each other* a longer notice period. If a cotenant violates this internal agreement, the remaining tenants can go after him in small claims court for the time (expressed as rent money) they were shorted. But the remaining tenants will still have to pay the full rent to the landlord as long as the departing tenant gave the landlord the statutorily required notice.

If there's a lease, the cotenant should either get permission from the landlord to leave early or, if this is impossible, find a new tenant acceptable to the landlord to take over. Again, if the cotenant has an understanding with her remaining cotenants that no one will leave without giving a longer notice period to the others, she'll have to deal with them if she splits early.

Unfortunately, cotenants often leave with not so much as a "good-bye," let alone a substitute. Here are the options for the ones left behind.

1. What to Do If You Want to Stay

Let's start with the worst-case scenario: Your cotenant leaves without the okay of the landlord. In this situation, the landlord has the option of evicting the rest of you, even if you can pay the full rent. How so? It goes back to joint and several liability: Moving out without the landlord's permission is a violation of a lease clause, and one cotenant's lease-breaking is a transgression for which all tenants are liable.

In practice, however, your landlord will probably let you stay if you're decent tenants and you can pay the rent. But if you're a troublesome group, he's likely to see this as a golden opportunity to be rid of you.

Hustle to cover the rent until you can replace your roommate. Your landlord may want to terminate your lease when the cotenant splits if he fears that you won't be able to cover the rent in the future. If you can assure the landlord that you can promptly bring in a good new cotenant, you might be able to salvage your tenancy. If you must, ask permission to pay the rent late or in installments. (See Chapter 3.) Or, ask the landlord to use the departed tenant's share of the security deposit to help pay the rent until you find an acceptable replacement.

Never bring in a new roommate without the landlord's consent. Moving in a new roommate without getting the approval of your landlord gives him a watertight reason to evict you, since your lease or rental agreement undoubtedly has a clause prohibiting unauthorized occupants.

2. What to Do If You Want to Move Out, Too

If your cotenant skips out, leaving you in the lurch, you may decide that you don't want to stay, either. To protect your security deposit and your good name at the credit bureau, follow these steps:

- If you are a month-to-month tenant, give the required amount of written notice (usually 30 days) immediately. Don't wait until you can't pay the next month's rent and receive a termination notice. (Chapter 9 shows how to give proper notice.)

- If you have a lease, let the landlord know in writing that you plan to move because you cannot afford the rent without your cotenant. Before you move, be extra accommodating when it comes to showing the unit to prospective renters. Facilitating a quick rerental is not just a courtesy to your landlord, but benefits you as well, since the sooner a new tenant takes over, the sooner your liability for the balance of the rent due under the lease ends. In addition, do your best to find an acceptable replacement tenant yourself. (See Chapter 9 for an explanation of the landlord's responsibility to look for a new tenant, and Section C, below, for advice on finding and presenting a replacement.)

C. Adding a New Roommate

If you want to add a roommate, most landlords will insist that the new roommate become a cotenant rather than a subtenant. Why? Unlike subtenants, cotenants are subject to joint and several liability, which allows the landlord to demand the entire rent from the cotenant as well as you. If it's up to you, on the other hand, in some situations you may want the newcomer to be a subtenant who rents from you and has no direct relationship with the landlord. For example, if you want to have the power to evict your new roommate, you'll need to set up a subtenancy, discussed in detail below in Section D.

Keep in mind that whether your roommate is a subtenant or a cotenant, you'll need the consent of the landlord.

1. Getting the Landlord's Approval

Obviously, you won't choose to live with someone who is financially unstable or inconsiderate. But even if you're satisfied with a prospective roommate's resume, your landlord might not be. There are a number of reasons a landlord might object to your chosen roommate, even if you've chosen someone who seems responsible and trustworthy. To increase your chances of an official okay, consider the following issues:

- **Will adding a roommate exceed the occupancy limit?** Landlords are entitled to set reasonable limits on the number of occupants per rental unit. (See Chapter 5, Section A.)
- **Will the new roommate meet your landlord's good-tenant criteria?** If your landlord subjected you to a thorough screening process, checking credit, employment, rental history, and references, put yourself in your landlord's loafers and do the same for your prospective roommate. If the results are dismal, don't waste your time further. If there's a smallish skeleton in the closet, do your best to prepare a plausible explanation.

2. Adding a Roommate to the Lease or Rental Agreement

If your intended roommate passes your landlord's credit and background checks, the landlord will probably ask both of you to sign a new lease or written month-to-month agreement. From your landlord's point of view, this is far more than a formality, since it makes the new arrival a cotenant who is 100% liable to pay rent and make good on any damage. It's also desirable from your perspective, because it makes it completely clear that your new roommate shares the same legal responsibilities that you do.

3. More Roommates, More Rent

If you add a roommate and sign a new rental agreement, technically speaking you're beginning a new tenancy, not changing an existing one. Consequently, if the landlord wants to increase the rent, the normal notice requirements for month-to-month tenancies (typically 30 days) don't apply and the rent may be increased as soon as you sign the new lease or rental agreement. The landlord may give you no notice other than presenting you with the new agreement containing the new rent provision. In that situation, the landlord can set the rent at whatever level he chooses (rent control areas excepted).

If you're adding a roommate to a lease, the same holds: Your landlord may increase the rent on the spot, since you're now beginning a new tenancy.

4. More Roommates, More Security Deposit

If you sign a new rental document, *all* bets are off, including the amount of the security deposit. If your state regulates the deposit in multiples of monthly rent, this is the only check on your landlord's ability to increase the deposit. Incidentally, the landlord can also change other lease clauses, such as those dealing with pets or late fees.

D. Taking in a Roomer

What if you're reluctant to share your entire home with a cotenant whom you have no power to evict, but want someone to share costs? The answer may be to take in a roomer as a subtenant.

When you take in a subtenant, you're that person's landlord. The main advantage of a subtenancy over a cotenancy is that it gives you the legal right to terminate the roomer's tenancy if things don't work out as planned. By contrast, you can't end the tenancy of a roommate who is a full-fledged cotenant—only your landlord can do this.

We suggest that you sign a month-to-month rental agreement with any subtenant, specifying rent and any restrictions on his use of your home. And, although your roomer doesn't sign the rental document you have with *your* landlord, he must comply with its rules as well as yours. Think of the arrangement as a set of nesting dolls: You live within your landlord's rules and regulations, and your subtenant lives within yours *and* the landlord's. So if your landlord prohibits using the pool after 10 p.m., you can't promise your roomer the joy of midnight swims. And, most important, if your roomer breaks your landlord's rules, the landlord may evict *you* to get rid of the roomer.

Don't get too enthusiastic about bringing someone in as a roomer until you get your landlord's approval. And be forewarned that many "landlords" in your position have problems getting a roomer to leave. You'll probably have to follow the same legal procedures all landlords use to terminate a tenancy.

RULES TO RENT BY

- **Choose your roommates carefully.** Cotenants are jointly and severally liable to the landlord, which means that each individual cotenant is legally responsible for complying with the lease terms, including payment of rent in full. To be blunt: When it comes to paying rent and making good on damage, you are your cotenant's guarantor—if she flakes, you pay.
- **What's between roommates is beyond the landlord.** Any agreements you make with your roommates aren't binding upon the landlord. Arrangements for splitting rent, paying utilities, or cleaning house don't affect each cotenant's joint and several liability to the landlord.
- **No midnight move-ins.** Any roommate changes should be approved by the landlord, especially the addition of new roommates. Landlord approval is necessary whether a new tenant becomes a cotenant or a subtenant.

Chapter 7

Repairs and Maintenance

In almost every state, you're entitled to a safe and livable home, regardless of how much rent you pay or whether your landlord tries to get you to accept a hovel. We're talking about basic, important items such as a roof that keeps out rain and snow, hot water, heat, and sturdy floors and walls that aren't in danger of imminent collapse. This list of necessary features includes the absence of significant danger from lead, asbestos, and, most recently, mold, plus reasonable protection from criminal intrusion. If the landlord refuses to provide or repair these aspects of your home, you may, depending on where you live, be able to:

- withhold rent
- pay for repairs yourself and deduct the cost from your rent
- sue the landlord, or
- move out without notice and without liability for future rent.

It's another ball game, however, when it comes to minor repairs such as clogged kitchen sinks, broken ovens, or leaky faucets. Unlike the big-ticket items mentioned above, minor repairs usually aren't directly addressed by state law. There are other legal ways, however, that you can get some action out of your landlord, as we'll explain in Section E, below.

If you've come to this chapter because you're bedeviled by a repair problem, help is at hand. Here's the drill:

- First, you must figure out whether your problem is, legally speaking, a "major" repair or a "minor" one.
- Second, having correctly classified your problem, you need to choose the appropriate course of action, from friendly persuasion to invoking legal remedies designed to empower tenants. *Many of the legal steps you can take to force a landlord to deal with a major repair will not work for a minor repair and can land you in legal hot water if used improperly.*
- Finally, you need to carry out the chosen strategy correctly. Usually, a necessary part of any plan will be to make sure that *you*

have fulfilled the tenant's responsibilities to use your rental with reasonable care.

TENANT TRAPS

Read this chapter to find out why you should:

- **Never agree to put up with a rental that lacks basic health and safety features** such as heat, plumbing, hot water, and weatherproofing. In most states, it is illegal for a landlord to offer a substandard rental or refuse to maintain a fit one.
- **Never push for repairs before figuring out whether it's a habitability problem or a minor repair.** Your bargaining power is vastly different depending on the seriousness of the problem.
- **Never delay in reporting major repair problems.**
- **Never use a "big stick" (such as rent withholding, discussed below) to prod your landlord into action without first telling her of the problem and giving her a reasonable time to fix it.**
- **Never use a big stick if you are behind in the rent, have an unauthorized roommate, or are violating some other important tenant obligation.**
- **Never make a big deal over a minor repair unless you are prepared for an uphill fight with your landlord.**

A. Your Right to a Livable Place

Your right to livable housing has a lofty-sounding legal name: You're entitled to the benefit of the landlord's "implied warranty of habitability." This means that, whether he knows it or not, your landlord has promised you a livable place simply by renting it to you. This basic right originated in court decisions in the early 1970s. By now, all but three states (Alabama, Arkansas, Colorado, and Indiana) have embraced this notion, either by decision from their highest court or by statute.

Tenants in Alabama, Arkansas, Colorado, and Indiana do have some rights to livable rentals. Although these states have not adopted the implied warranty on a statewide level, many local governments within them (cities and counties) have enacted ordinances that come close to establishing the same standards. Check your local housing laws (found in most public libraries or online) for details. (Appendix 1 shows you how to find statutes online.)

So what does it mean to say that your landlord is expected to fulfill an implied warranty of habitability? It means he must:

- keep basic structural elements of the building, including floors, stairs, walls, and roofs, safe and intact
- maintain all common areas, such as hallways and stairways, in a safe and clean condition
- keep electrical, plumbing, sanitary, heating, ventilating, and air-conditioning systems and elevators operating safely
- supply cold and hot water and heat in reasonable amounts at reasonable times
- provide trash receptacles and arrange for trash pick-up
- manage known environmental toxins such as lead paint dust and asbestos so that they don't pose a significant danger
- in most states, provide rental property that is reasonably safe from the threat of foreseeable criminal intrusions, and
- exterminate infestations of rodents and other vermin.

In virtually every state (Texas and Maine excepted), these rights are yours, no matter what the landlord has asked you to sign or agree to. In other words, the landlord cannot shrug off these responsibilities in a "disclaimer" when the tenancy begins. And he can't effectively ask you to waive your right to them. (Any so-called waiver will not be upheld by a court.)

⚠️ **Don't wait until you move in to discover major repair problems.** Always inspect the rental unit—and have the landlord do necessary repairs—before you move in, as recommended in Chapter 2.

IF AT FIRST THE LANDLORD DOESN'T SUCCEED, HE MUST KEEP TRYING

Some habitability problems can be addressed with decisiveness: A malfunctioning heater can normally be fixed with new parts and/or service, or a lead-based paint problem can be tackled with an appropriate abatement plan. But what about persistent problems that just won't go away despite the landlord's efforts—for example, roaches in an older urban building that are firmly entrenched and resistant to repeated exterminations? The answer is that the landlord must keep trying. In the meantime, assuming the problem has made the rental legally unlivable, you have the right to move out, as explained below in Section D.

---

1. Major Habitability Problems Versus Minor Problems

As you look over the above list of repairs and maintenance that make up the landlord's duty to provide fit housing, you can see why these are called major, not minor, issues. When they pop up, a reasonable occupant would be concerned for her health or safety. Put another way, a reasonable person wouldn't freely choose to live in a place with any of these problems. On the other hand, a minor repair is annoying, limiting, or distasteful—and it may be close to driving you nuts—but it wouldn't seriously endanger the health or safety of a reasonable tenant. The chart below gives more examples of major versus minor repair problems.

CLASSIFYING YOUR REPAIR PROBLEM

It is essential that you correctly classify your repair problem—major or minor—before approaching your landlord or taking stronger measures. Following are some concrete examples of the two types of problems. The test for every repair problem is: Does this make my rental unfit to live in? If so, it's major; if not, it's minor.

MAJOR REPAIR	**MINOR REPAIR**
A roof leak that results in a wall of mildew in the bedroom	A roof leak that has caused a slight stain in the ceiling plaster in the hallway
A totally broken hot water heater	A hot water heater that heats to five degrees less than the temperature required by state statute
A furnace that won't turn on	A furnace that clanks and creaks when the fan runs
A front door that will not lock	A screen door (in front of a door that locks) with a broken latch
A toilet that won't flush in a one-bathroom rental	A toilet that flushes poorly in a two-bath unit
A lobby that is filled with tenants' garbage because the landlord has failed to provide trash bins and has not arranged for pick-up	A lobby that's in need of a good vacuuming and paint job
A broken heater during the winter	A broken heater in the summer during a warm spell
An apartment rented to a family with young children where there is deteriorating lead paint	An apartment with faded and dirty latex paint

⚠ A defect is "minor" not because of its cost, but because it doesn't make your rental uninhabitable. For example, if the only thing between you and a heated apartment is a $50 furnace part, the repair is "major", because an unheated home is unlivable. If the landlord refuses to fix it, you can use the "big stick" remedies explained in Section D, below. On the other hand, replacing an ugly but otherwise safe carpet may cost thousands, but it is a "minor" repair, because floor coverings that are merely shabby do not make your home unfit.

LEAD AND ASBESTOS

When lead-based paint dust and asbestos fibers are inhaled, they can cause significant health problems. Dangerous levels of either toxin can make your rental unlivable and usually constitute a violation of the implied warranty of habitability.

Federal law has stepped in to require landlords at least to warn tenants of the presence of lead dust and asbestos. In addition, if you are injured by one of these toxins and can show that your landlord knew of its presence, you may be able to sue for your injuries.

Lead. A federal law known as Title X ("Ten") of the United States Code requires landlords of pre-1978 buildings to tell every new tenant about the presence of lead-based paint if the landlord knows it's on the property. (42 U.S. Code § 4852d.) Your landlord should have given you a disclosure form and the government booklet "Protect Your Family From Lead in Your Home" when you signed the lease or rental agreement. Federal law does not, at this time, require the landlord to test for lead paint dust. In addition to the federal rules, many state laws impose maintenance and remediation duties, which may involve covering the lead-based paint or carefully removing it. For more information on Title X, contact the National Lead Information Center at 800-424-LEAD, or go to their website at www.nsc.org/ehc/lead.htm. To learn whether your state has laws in this field, contact your state's consumer protection agency.

Asbestos. Asbestos fibers that have begun to break down (from the passage of time or by being disturbed through repair work) will enter the air and pose health risks to those who breathe them. Under regulations imposed by the U.S. Occupational Safety and Health Administration (OSHA), owners of buildings constructed before 1981 must install warning labels, train staff, and notify people who work in areas that might contain asbestos. (29 Code of Federal Regulations (C.F.R.) §§ 1910.1001 and following.) Although these rules are designed to protect workers, they are also a boon to tenants, because once your landlord learns about the presence of airborne asbestos fibers, he's on notice of a dangerous situation. If he fails to take action (by encapsulating the asbestos, for example), he risks a costly lawsuit if one of his tenants is injured. The landlord generally does not have to take action if the asbestos is intact and is not entering the airstream. For further information on asbestos rules, inspections, and control, contact the nearest office of the U.S. Occupational Safety and Health Administration (OSHA) or call the national office at 202-219-8148. You can also learn more by visiting the OSHA website at www.osha.gov.

2. What *Exactly* Does "Fit and Habitable" Mean?

Chances are you aren't yet satisfied with our description of the implied warranty of habitability. If your repair problem is clearly a big deal (no heat in South Dakota in December), no one's going to argue with you. But often the line between major and minor isn't so clear. To better place your problem in the right category, you'll have to go to the source of your state's implied warranty—a state code or statute or, in some states, a court decision. Your local government (city or county) may also have ordinances that establish habitability requirements. If so, you may find that there are specifics (such as a minimum hot water temperature) that can help you label your problem.

This section discusses what these laws typically require of a landlord. Then, in Section C, below, we'll show you what you can do to encourage your landlord to comply. And if you have to get heavy (by withholding the rent or repairing the problem and deducting the cost from your rent), we'll show you how in Section D, below.

a.   Local Ordinances

City or county building or housing codes regulate structural aspects of buildings and usually set specific space standards, such as the minimum size of sleeping rooms. They also establish minimum requirements for light and ventilation, sanitation and sewage disposal, heating, water supply (such as how hot the water must be), fire protection, wiring (such as the number of electrical outlets per room), and security devices such as locks.

Most local housing codes also prohibit "nuisances." A nuisance is something that is dangerous to human life or detrimental to health or morals—for example, overcrowding a room with occupants or providing insufficient ventilation, illumination, or sewage capacity. Drug dealing on the premises is also a legal nuisance, since it invariably involves the comings and goings of a criminal element with a potential for unhealthy violence.

Contact your local building, housing, health, and/or fire departments for information on the exact requirements your landlord must meet.

b.   State Housing Codes

Many states have general laws requiring landlords to keep rental units fit. These laws are usually less detailed than local codes, but in some states they're rather specific—some have statewide door and window lock laws, for example. To find our whether your state has any laws in this area:

- Go to your local law library (or go online) and check your land-lord-tenant statutes. We've listed the statute numbers by state in Appendix 1, where we also explain how to find them online.

- Look in the index of your state codes for subentries under Landlord-Tenant, such as "Duty to Maintain" or "Repairs."
- Contact your state's consumer protection agency and ask for any informational booklets.

The statute that sets out the specific requirements for a habitable building usually won't tell you what to do if yours doesn't measure up. Your legal recourse (called your legal "remedy") is usually found with other landlord-tenant statutes, and sometimes in the code sections that deal with unlawful detainer (eviction) procedures. (Below, in Section D, we go into these remedies in detail.)

WHO'S RESPONSIBLE FOR CRIME?

Landlords are increasingly held accountable for criminal incidents that they should have foreseen and taken reasonable steps to avoid. Buildings that are crime-ridden or open invitations to criminals might qualify as uninhabitable, though the willingness of state courts to reach this conclusion varies widely. If your state considers a vulnerable building to be a violation of the implied warranty of habitability, you may be able to pressure your landlord to address the problems by using one of the tenant remedies discussed below in Section D.

If your building or neighborhood has had recent break-ins, your landlord's duty to take reasonable precautions (such as better lighting, locks, and perhaps a doorman) goes up. However, courts will usually not hold landlords responsible for an isolated incident; nor will they expect landlords to erect virtual moats around their property. And remember: You, too, bear some responsibility for your own safety. A tenant who foolishly courts danger in a high-crime neighborhood will find little sympathy with most juries.

B. Your Repair and Maintenance Responsibilities

Your landlord isn't the only one with responsibilities to keep the rental unit reasonably maintained. State and local laws require you, the tenant, to keep house a certain way, as the list below demonstrates.

Now, you may be wondering what your housekeeping responsibilities have to do with major repairs that are on the shoulders of the landlord. The answer is that if a major habitability problem is the result of *your* not keeping up your end of the maintenance bargain, you cannot expect the landlord to pay for the repair, and you cannot use any of the tenant remedies, such as rent withholding, to accomplish the job. For example, if your only toilet is clogged because your babysitter tried to flush a diaper, it's a habitability problem, true, but the cost of repairing it will fall squarely on you.

You are obligated to:

- Keep your rental unit as clean and safe as the condition of the premises permits.
- Dispose of garbage, rubbish, and other waste in a clean and safe manner.
- Keep plumbing fixtures as clean as their condition permits.
- Use electrical, plumbing, sanitary, heating, ventilating, air-conditioning, and other facilities and other systems, including elevators, properly.
- Fix things you break or damage.
- In many states, notify the landlord promptly of defective or dangerous conditions on the property.

Your landlord can't, however, charge you for problems caused by normal wear and tear—for example, a carpet that has worn out from years of use. (Chapter 9 discusses the difference between normal wear and tear and damage.)

Knowing about—and fulfilling—your own responsibilities as a tenant makes you more than just a virtuous renter. The dividends of living up to your duties include the confidence that:

- You can expect a positive reference from this landlord when you move on to the next rental.

- You are well positioned should you need to ask an occasional favor, such as paying the rent late or letting your sister stay with you for a month while she looks for her own place.

- You can withhold rent or use a repair and deduct statute (if your state allows these remedies), which usually may not be used if the tenant is in violation of a lease clause or other important tenant responsibility.

C. Persuading Your Landlord to Do Major Repairs

Suppose now that you're comfortable that you have correctly classified the problem you're living with as a major one. But it's one thing to have the law on your side—it's often quite another to get your landlord to abide by it. Here are some tips for getting results, short of hauling out the big guns like rent withholding or repair-and-deduct. If this approach doesn't get results, head for Section D, below.

- **Put your repair request in writing.** Be as specific as possible regarding the problem, its effect on you, what you want done, and when. This will get your landlord's attention better than a casual chat on the stairs. It will also be important proof that you gave your landlord "notice" of the problem, a step you must take in case you have to resort to a self-help remedy such as repair-and-deduct. Of course, if it's an emergency, call first and then follow up in writing.

- **Put the landlord's promises in writing, too.** If the landlord agrees on a requested repair, follow up with a letter confirming his promise. (This is called a letter of understanding, which we explain in Chapter 2, Section G.) If he doesn't write back, he has legally committed himself to your version of his promise. This may come in handy if he later reneges on the plan and you need to take self-help steps.

- **Emphasize the dire consequences.** If the repair problem poses a safety threat, it won't hurt to point that out to the landlord in your written request for repairs. For example, a broken lock will make it easy for a burglar to enter, and a loose carpet edge is an accident waiting to happen. Even the laziest landlord will take care of business if he senses that a lawsuit may be on the horizon. The Sample Request for Repairs, below, shows how a tenant might phrase her request.

- **Strength in numbers.** If you're not the only one living with a major problem—such as poor building-wide security or lack of heat—gather forces and present your request as a group. The specter of multiple tenants complaining to the building inspector or withholding rent often gets results.

SAMPLE REQUEST FOR REPAIRS

May 3, 200X

Ms. Lisa Bilding
23 Oakmont Street
City Center, MD 55555

Dear Ms. Bilding,

As you know, I am your tenant at 57 Washington Street, City Center. I spoke to you last night about a serious problem with the hot water in my flat. Yesterday I discovered that the water temperature had suddenly risen quite high—in fact, it is practically scalding. I've attempted to adjust the thermostat, but it doesn't do any good.

While I have been careful to open the cold tap at the same time as the hot when I use any sink, I am concerned that my children will forget to do so and may be burned by the very hot water. I would very much appreciate it if you could attend to this problem as quickly as possible. Please contact me at one of the numbers below so that I can arrange to be there when you (or a repairperson) come to work on the water heater.

Yours truly,
R.U. Lisning, Tenant
57 Washington Street
Home: 301-555-4546
Work: 301-555-5432

D.   Using Heavy Artillery for Major Repairs

If, despite your businesslike requests, the landlord hasn't fixed or addressed a serious problem that truly makes your rental unit uninhabitable—rats in the kitchen, for example—you will want to take stronger measures. Your options include one or more of what we call the "big sticks" in a tenant's arsenal. Big stick remedies include:

- calling state or local building or health inspectors
- withholding the rent
- repairing the problem, or having it repaired by a professional, and deducting the cost from your rent (called "repair-and-deduct")
- moving out, or
- paying the rent and then suing the landlord for the difference between the rent you paid and the value of the defective premises.

It's important to understand that you shouldn't use a big stick remedy rashly. Before you withhold rent, move out, or adopt another extreme remedy, make sure every one of these conditions is met:

- The problem is serious, not just annoying, and imperils your health or safety. Not every building code violation or annoying defect in your rental home justifies use of a "big stick" against the landlord.
- You (or a guest) did not cause the problem, either deliberately or through carelessness or neglect. If so, you can't pursue big stick options.
- You told the landlord about the problem and gave him a reasonable opportunity—or the minimum amount of notice required by state law—to get it fixed. You can't use big stick options without taking these first steps. You'll need to check your state's law for the exact notification requirements for the specific option you are pursuing.
- As a tenant, you are squeaky clean. Under most rent withholding laws you cannot withhold rent if you are behind in the rent or in violation of an important lease clause.

- You are willing to risk termination of your tenancy by an annoyed landlord. Exercising any of the rights discussed here will not endear you to your landlord. Many states forbid your landlord from retaliating against you by raising the rent or terminating your tenancy, but, unfortunately, some states don't. If your lease is about to run out (or you're a month-to-month tenant) and your state does not protect you from retaliatory rent increases or evictions, a complaint to health inspectors or the use of a big stick could end up causing you to lose your rental. (See the Chapter 11 discussion on retaliation and "State Laws Prohibiting Landlord Retaliation" in Appendix 2.)

- You are willing to risk eviction if a judge decides that you shouldn't have used the big stick, and your credit rating can bear this negative mark. Even if you're sure that you were justified in using a big stick, a judge may decide otherwise. For example, if you withhold rent, the landlord may sue to evict you based on nonpayment of rent. In most states and in most situations, you'll have a second chance to pay the balance before being evicted, but not always. For some tenants, additional negative marks on their credit records will cause extremely serious problems not only for future rentals but for loans and employment as well.

- You can find a comparable or better unit if you move out, either voluntarily or because the building is closed due to code violations you have reported. In some states, landlords whose buildings are closed due to code violations must help their tenants with relocation expenses.

Before doing repairs yourself, withholding rent, or using another "big stick," make sure you have proof of how bad the situation was. Take pictures of the problem or ask a reputable and impartial contractor or repairperson to examine the defect and give you a written, signed, and dated description of the problem and an estimate for repair.

1. Reporting Code Violations to Housing Inspectors

If the problem you're facing is a violation of a state or local housing law, you may contact the agency in charge of enforcing the law. This may be a housing or building agency or a health or fire department. The inspector will investigate and give the landlord a notice of violation and a deadline, typically 30 to 60 days, to correct the problem. The deadline may be shortened for extremely serious violations.

A landlord's failure to abide by the correction order may result in fines and even imprisonment. Keep in mind that there is wild variation in the actual effectiveness of inspectors, depending on their workloads and budgets. In some large cities, landlords have learned to evade and postpone. But fear not: You have more arrows in your quiver.

⚠️ **Health, fire, or building inspectors may order the building closed.** If the problem you report is extremely serious, the inspectors may close your building and order all tenants to leave, sometimes on very short notice. Typically, you won't even have a chance to voice your objections. Think carefully and plan ahead if there's a chance that your phone call could result in actually worsening your living situation.

2. Withholding the Rent

If your landlord has not met the responsibility of keeping your unit livable, you may be able to stop paying any rent to the landlord until the repairs are made. This is called rent withholding. Many states have established rent withholding, either by statute or court decision. (See "State Laws on Rent Withholding and Repair-and-Deduct" in Appendix 2.) Rent withholding can be done *only* in states that specifically allow it by law. If yours isn't one of them, you'll have to use another approach.

The term "withholding" is actually a bit misleading, since in some states and cities you can't simply keep the rent money until your landlord fixes the problem. Instead, you often have to deposit the withheld rent with a court, a neutral third party, or an escrow account set up by a local court or housing agency until the repairs are accomplished. (And even if your statute doesn't require it, it's a good idea to escrow the rent yourself, as explained below.)

In states that have not established an escrow scheme, your right to withhold the rent is somewhat indirect: When you don't pay the rent and the landlord tries to evict you (which she surely will), the statute allows you to argue in your defense that you didn't owe any rent because the unit was unfit. If the judge or jury believes you, you will win the eviction lawsuit and will be allowed to stay.

⚠️ **Never reduce the rent unless your state law authorizes rent withholding, either directly (by escrowing) or as a defense to an eviction.** If you do, you can expect a speedily delivered termination notice, followed by an eviction lawsuit, for nonpayment of rent. Your theory—that the landlord was entitled to less rent because the premises weren't livable—is not likely to be well received in a state that hasn't taken the issue seriously enough to establish orderly procedures (rent withholding) that will pressure landlords into providing habitable housing. If you lose, you'll lose your rented home. Instead, use one of the other remedies mentioned here, including repair and deduct (if available), moving out, or filing a lawsuit in small claims court asking for a retroactive rent reduction for substandard conditions.

Before you can properly withhold the rent, remember that all of these requirements must be met:

- The lack of maintenance or repair has made your dwelling unlivable. (Section A, above, discusses habitability requirements.)
- The problems were not caused by you or your guest, either deliberately or through neglect.
- You told the landlord about the problem and gave him a reasonable time to fix it or the minimum amount required by state law.
- You are not behind on the rent or in violation of a lease or rental agreement clause.

a. How to Withhold Rent

Needless to say, when your landlord gets a short rent check, he won't be pleased. He may terminate your tenancy for nonpayment of rent and file for eviction if you don't pay up (or move). You'll survive the eviction action if you've used the withholding remedy correctly *and* you have good proof to back you up. And, let's face it—you'll need a bit of luck, since even a solid case can't overcome an ignorant or biased judge.

Here are the steps to follow if you decide to withhold the rent.

Step 1: Research the law. If rent withholding is allowed in your state, the statute (law) will be listed in Appendix 2. Also, check if any local laws apply. In a few localities subject to rent control, the procedure may be part of your local ordinance. Read the law to find out:

- what circumstances justify rent withholding
- whether you must give the landlord a certain amount of notice (ten to 30 days are typical) to fix the defect, or whether the response time must simply be "reasonable" under the circumstances, and
- whether you must place the unpaid rent in a separate bank account or deposit it with a court or local housing agency.

Step 2: Notify your landlord. Give your landlord written notice of the problem and your intent to withhold rent. Refer to your state's law or statute that allows withholding and include a copy of it. Give your landlord a reasonable deadline. Send the letter certified and ask for a "return receipt."

Step 3: Collect evidence. In case your landlord tries to evict you for nonpayment of rent, you will want to prepare your defense from day one. You'll want to keep copies of all correspondence with the landlord, plus photographs of the problem.

Step 4: Repeat your request for repairs. If the landlord hasn't responded satisfactorily to your first letter, give the landlord one last deadline— say, 48 hours or whatever period you feel is reasonable under the circumstances.

Step 5: File any court papers. Under some state laws, you must ask a local court for permission to withhold rent, provide compelling reasons why your rental is not livable, and follow specific procedures. You can get the necessary information and forms from the court or housing department that is named in your rent withholding statute.

Step 6: Deposit your rent in escrow. In some states, you may have to deposit your rent with the specified local court or housing agency or in a separate bank account. Even if your statute does not require this, we recommend that you deposit the withheld rent into an escrow account held by a neutral third party. This will dispel any suggestion that you are withholding rent simply in order to avoid paying it.

If a court or housing department is not set up to handle withheld rent, try asking a mediation service if it will establish an account for this purpose. Or ask your attorney to deposit the withheld rent in her "trust account." You can also set up a separate bank account of your own and use it only for withheld rent.

b.   What Happens to the Withheld Rent

If the rent money is being held by a court or housing authority, landlords can sometimes ask for release of some of the withheld rent to pay for repairs. While repairs are being made, you may continue to pay the entire rent to the court or housing authority, or you may be directed to pay some rent to the landlord and the balance to the court or housing authority. When the dwelling is certified as fit by the local housing authorities or the court, any money in the account is returned to the landlord, minus court costs and inspection fees.

If your withholding law does not require you to escrow the rent and a court has not been involved, you and the landlord are free to make your own arrangements as to the distribution of the money. Once your landlord has made the repairs, he will probably expect full payment of the withheld rent. If you don't pay up, you can expect your landlord to file an eviction lawsuit for nonpayment of rent.

Understandably, you may not feel like paying full rent, in retrospect, for the months you spent living in a substandard home while politely trying to convince the landlord to take care of business. In short, you may want a retroactive reduction in rent, starting from the time that the premises became uninhabitable. (Some states will limit you to a reduction starting from the time you notified the landlord of the habitability problem.) Reducing the rent after the fact is known in legalese as rent "abatement." You may get a retroactive rent abatement through a court process or through negotiation with your landlord.

Don't pay full fare for a substandard unit. Ask your landlord or the court to fix the rent at what a unit with these defects would have rented for on the open market; compare this sum to your stated rent, and argue that you deserve the difference. Or, if the defect rendered a portion of the rental unusable (a leak in the living room, for example), estimate what percentage of the rental was affected and reduce the rent accordingly.

3. Making Repairs and Deducting the Cost: "Repair-and-Deduct"

Depending on where you live, you may be eligible to use another powerful legal remedy called "repair-and-deduct." Over half the states and some large cities allow it. (See "State Laws on Rent Withholding and Repair-and-Deduct" in Appendix 2.) If your state doesn't allow repair-and-deduct, check your local housing ordinances to determine whether your city has independently adopted it. *If your state or city does not have a repair-and-deduct statute, this procedure is not available to you.*

It works like this: If you have tried and failed to get the landlord to fix a serious defect, you can hire a repair person to fix it or fix it yourself and subtract the cost from the following month's rent. The statute will usually specify:

- the circumstances justifying your use of the remedy (usually only habitability problems can be addressed with repair-and-deduct)

- the amount of rent you can use for repairs (such as one month's rent), and
- the frequency with which you can use the remedy (once in an 18-month period, for example).

The repair-and-deduct remedy is a poor choice when it comes to big-ticket projects such as a major roof repair. Obviously, if you're limited to a twice-a-year expenditure of half your monthly rent, you are not going to be able to pay for a $20,000 roof job. Sometimes, however, a number of tenants might pool their dollar limits to accomplish a costly repair.

4. Moving Out

If your dwelling isn't habitable and hasn't been made so despite your complaints and repair requests, you also have the right to move out—either temporarily or permanently. You can also move out if the landlord has tried but failed to remedy the problem. For example, unsuccessful attempts to rid a building of vermin infestations entitle you to leave—even if the landlord has tried his best to fix the problem.

These drastic measures are justified only when there are truly serious problems, such as the lack of essential services, the total or partial destruction of the premises, or the presence of environmental health hazards such as asbestos or lead paint dust.

If you have time remaining on a lease and use this remedy improperly (for an insignificant problem, for example), you risk losing your security deposit or even being sued for the remainder of the rent due under the lease. Therefore, check your state law for details, which may include:

- whether you must first call the building inspectors
- how much time you must give your landlord to fix the problem, and
- the amount of notice, if any, you must provide before moving out.

Consider a temporary move. If your landlord learns that you are serious about abandoning ship, you might suggest that she pay for temporary lodging while the problem is fixed. After all, from her point of view, this is cheaper in the long run than losing a rent-paying tenant and trying to rerent a substandard place. In some states, landlords *must* pay for temporary housing while court-ordered repairs are made, typically when lead paint problems are being remedied.

5. Suing the Landlord

A consumer who purchases a product—be it a car, a hair dryer, or a steak dinner—is justified in expecting a minimum level of quality and is entitled to compensation if the product is seriously flawed. The same goes for tenants. Except in Alabama, Arkansas, Colorado, and Indiana (where the implied warranty of habitability is not recognized on a state level), if your rental is not habitable you can sue the landlord—whether or not you move out. You can probably use small claims court, which allows claims of up to several thousand dollars. You won't need to hire a lawyer. (Chapter 13, Section C, discusses small claims court procedures.)

Suing the landlord makes sense only if you can safely continue to live in your rental. For example, if the roof leaks only into the second bedroom and you can move the kids into the living room for a while, you might want to stay and sue in order to avoid the hassle of moving, arranging for the repair yourself (repair-and-deduct), or figuring out the complications of rent withholding. But you wouldn't want to stay and sue if you are without heat in the winter or in danger of electrocution every time you turn on the lights.

What are the pros and cons of suing your landlord instead of using repair-and-deduct or rent withholding? On the positive side, if you lose your lawsuit you'll have lost some time and money, but you won't be evicted, as can happen with the unsuccessful use of repair-and-deduct or rent withholding. But suing isn't entirely risk-free, especially if you're a month-to-month tenant or nearing the end of a lease you would like to renew. Your annoyed landlord may simply decide to terminate or not renew. Tenants who are protected by state antiretaliation laws will have some protection, but to assert your rights you'll have to bring a lawsuit, a dreary prospect. (Landlord retaliation is covered in Chapter 11.)

In your lawsuit, you ask the judge to rule that your unrepaired rental was not worth what you've paid for it. You want to be paid the difference between the monthly rent and the real value of the unit, times the number of months that you've lived with the substandard conditions. In short, you'll ask for a retroactive rent decrease—rent "abatement" in legalese. In addition, you can sue your landlord for lost or damaged property (for example, furniture ruined by water leaking through the roof).

In some states, you may also ask the court for an order directing the landlord to repair the defects, with rent reduced until they are fixed. In others, small claims courts can only order the landlord to pay you for your losses, but usually the money judgment gets the landlord's attention and he makes the repairs.

E. Laying the Minor Repair Job on the Landlord

Until now, this chapter has focused on major repairs: how to know what they are and how to get them fixed. But that may not be what's troubling you. In fact, ask a group of tenants which rental problems are most annoying and chances are you'll hear a recitation of day-to-day but nonetheless important problems that everyone encounters now and then: leaky faucets, malfunctioning appliances, worn carpets, noisy heaters, and dozens of other frustrating breakdowns.

Unfortunately, if your landlord refuses to attend to minor repairs, you can't withhold rent, move out, or use most of the other "big stick" legal weapons discussed in Section D, above. Even so, there are several proven strategies for getting results.

1. Ways to Put the Problem on the Landlord

There are a number of legal theories that you can use to place a minor repair responsibility on the landlord's shoulders. Here are several. Then we'll turn in Section F, below to how you can put these theories to work.

a. Building Codes

State and local building codes mainly concern structural requirements such as roofs and flooring and essential services like hot water. If your repair problem is also a significant violation of the building code, you may be dealing with a habitability problem that can be addressed using one of the remedies explained above in Section D. But some codes also regulate lesser aspects of your rental, such as the number of electrical outlets. Check your state's building code and any local ordinances to see whether your problem fits within them. If it does, you might get some results from the governmental agency that administers the codes, as explained below in Section F.

b. Landlord-Tenant Laws

Some states place the responsibility for some minor repairs directly on the landlord. Check your state's statutes, which you'll find listed in "Landlord-Tenant Statutes" in Appendix 2. Note that in many states, renters of single-family homes may agree to take on responsibilities that would belong to the landlord in a multiunit setting.

c. Promises in the Lease

You may need to look no further than your own lease or rental agreement to find that the landlord has, perhaps unwittingly, promised to fix your problem. Even a simple list of the amenities that come with the rental—such as a dishwasher, sauna, or washing machine—constitutes an implied promise that the landlord will provide them in a *workable* condition.

d.   Promises in Ads

If an advertisement for your unit described or listed a feature, such as a swimming pool, that significantly affected your decision to move into the particular rental unit, you have the right to hold the landlord to these promises—as long as the breakdown is not your fault. (See Section 2, below.) The promise doesn't have to be in words—a glossy photo showing a pool constitutes an obligation that the landlord will provide one (and keep it up). And the promise may be oral, made during rental negotiations. ("You'll love our four-court tennis area!") The landlord who turns the tennis court into a parking lot will do so at some expense if his tenants are savvy—read on.

e.   Implied Promises

Finally, you may be faced with a minor repair problem that doesn't fit within any of the above ways to nail the landlord: no code or law violation, no promise to fix it in the lease, no promise in an ad or during an enthusiastic prerental tour. Still, something was working or in good repair when you moved in and has since deteriorated. What's your theory now?

It's rather simple: You are entitled to get what you pay for. Many courts will hold a landlord legally responsible for maintaining all significant aspects of your rental unit. If you rent a unit that already has certain features—light fixtures that work, doors that open and close smoothly, faucets that don't leak, tile that doesn't fall off the wall—many judges reason that the landlord has made an implied contract to keep them in workable order throughout your tenancy.

The flip side of this principle is that if you pay for a hamburger, the waiter doesn't have to deliver a steak. In other words, if your rental was shabby when you moved in and the landlord never gave you reason to believe that it would be spruced up, you have no legal right to demand improvements—unless, of course, you can show health hazards or code violations. As when you buy secondhand goods "as is" for a low price, legally you are stuck with your deal. (But Section F, below, suggests some strategies—based on subtly showing your landlord the consequences of ignoring minor repairs—that may convince a reluctant landlord to take better care of the property.)

Another way to show that your landlord has made an implied promise to attend to this repair is his past conduct. If your landlord has consistently fixed or maintained a particular feature of your rental, he has made an implied promise to continue doing so. For example, if he's regularly fixed the finicky timer on the hot tub but suddenly decides that he's had enough, you may point to his past efforts as establishing a promise to continue to fix the tub.

2. Your Responsibilities for Minor Repairs

All tenants are responsible for keeping their units in a clean, safe condition and reimbursing the landlord for damage they might cause. (These duties are explained in more detail in Section B, above.) Many leases also prohibit tenants from making alterations or improvements without the landlord's consent.

These rules often work in tandem. If you damage the garbage disposal by dropping a piece of silverware into it, you'll have to pay for replacing the disposal, but you'll need your landlord's okay before you hire the plumber. Minor repairs that are caused by normal wear and tear, however, are the landlord's responsibility.

F. Getting the Landlord to Make Minor Repairs

By now you should have a pretty good idea as to whether or not your landlord is legally responsible for fixing the particular minor problem that is bedeviling you. Your next job is to get the landlord to do it. First, try for some cooperation. If he won't budge, it may be time to take a confrontational approach.

THINK BEFORE YOU LEAP

If you have a month-to-month tenancy, in most states your landlord can terminate your tenancy with just 30 days' notice, without having to give a reason. And if your lease is about to expire and you'd like a renewal, the landlord can likewise simply decline to offer it. (Rent control ordinances may restrict the landlord; see Chapter 12.)

The ease with which your landlord can get rid of you means you should think twice before trying one of the adversarial strategies discussed below—reporting your landlord for building code violations or suing in small claims court—over minor problems with your rental.

An antiretaliation law, if one is in force where you live, may protect you from a termination or nonrenewal. (Retaliation is discussed in Chapter 11.) But if you have to go to court to argue about it, spending precious time away from work or your free time, you may end up wishing you'd never complained about that cracked mirror.

---

1. Appealing to the Landlord

Chances are your oral pleas have been met with delays or refusals. Now it's time to write a request, keeping in mind your landlord's guiding lights: making money, avoiding tenant hassles, and staying out of legal hot water. An appeal designed to further *his* concerns is likely to succeed.

If possible, write your letter using one or more of the following approaches:

- It's a small problem now, but likely to get bigger (the landlord reads: less expensive to deal with it now).
- There is potential for injury (the landlord reads: a personal injury lawsuit in the making).

- There is a security problem that imperils your safety (another lawsuit).
- The problem affects many tenants (oh no! many lawsuits!).
- You'd be more than happy to fix it yourself, but it's clear you don't know the difference between a chisel and a screwdriver (a botched job that could be ruinous).

Often, even the most stingy and dense landlord will spring to action when he sees that the results of not taking care of business could be worse than dealing with your request now.

2. Reporting Code Violations

If the problem you want fixed constitutes a code violation, such as low water pressure, you might find an ally in the building or housing agency in charge of enforcing the code. Whether you'll get any action out of the agency will depend on the seriousness of the violation, the workload of the agency, and its ability to enforce its compliance orders. Since by definition your problem is minor, don't expect lots of help if code enforcement officials are already overworked.

3. Suing in Small Claims Court

If you can reasonably argue that you aren't getting what you paid for, you might decide to sue in small claims court. But before you do, write a demand letter stating what you want and that you intend to sue if necessary. Write a second letter if you don't get results.

If the second letter doesn't do the trick, it's time to head for the small claims court clerk's office. We know of one tenant who successfully sued her landlord for failing to repair a dishwasher that was functioning when she moved in. In her lawsuit, she calculated how much time she spent hand-washing the dishes each day, multiplied that figure times the number of days she had been without the dishwasher, and multiplied that figure by her state's minimum wage. She won.

(See Chapter 13, Section C, for more advice on how to prepare a small claims court case.)

⚠ **Don't withhold rent.** If you do, you invite an eviction lawsuit. (The only time to withhold rent is when following a statutory withholding process, described in Section D, above.) Instead, ask for a retroactive rent abatement (or reduction) in your lawsuit which, if granted, will accomplish the same thing without the risk of an eviction lawsuit.

RULES TO RENT BY

- **Never agree to rent a substandard unit.** Your landlord is breaking the law, and you can expect nothing but trouble.
- **Remember your own duties as a tenant**—keeping your unit clean and safe and paying for any damage you or your guest may cause.
- **Put all repair requests in writing and keep a copy for your files** along with all correspondence with the landlord—you may need evidence later to prove that you told the landlord about the problem.
- **Use a letter of understanding to document your landlord's promise to do a repair.** It will commit him to the promise unless he writes back and disputes your version.
- **Be certain** that you are paid up in rent and not in violation of any major lease clause before using the "big stick" remedies of rent withholding or repair-and-deduct.
- **Think twice before launching a campaign for a minor repair.** If you are not protected by antiretaliation laws, you may win the battle but lose the war (your tenancy).

Chapter 8

Tenants' Rights to Privacy

You may have already encountered a landlord who cannot stop fussing over the property or who frequently tries to wangle an invitation into your home to look around. Even worse are landlords and managers who use a passkey to enter without notice when you're not at home and there is no emergency. The idea that a landlord might at any time violate your private space and even go through your personal belongings is very upsetting.

This chapter covers your basic rights to privacy and what to do about a landlord or manager who violates these rights. You can sue your landlord for entering unlawfully—but it's rarely worth the time or trouble. Unfortunately, the law won't solve all problems inherent in dealing with difficult people. In some instances, you may find that you'll either have to grimace and bear the actions of an intrusive landlord or move on.

💡 **Get the low-down on the landlord before you sign up.** Talk to neighbors or the tenant whose unit you're considering: Is this a nosy landlord? If so, look elsewhere.

TENANT TRAPS

Read this chapter to find out why you should:

- **Never sign a lease or rental agreement waiving your rights to privacy.** Many courts will refuse to uphold such a waiver, but you'll have to spend many miserable hours fighting with your landlord and arguing in court before that lesson will be pounded into your landlord. Besides, any landlord who wants to do business this way is likely to be a sleaze in other respects, too.

- **Never complain to your landlord about privacy violations without putting the complaint in writing (in a follow-up letter after a conversation, if necessary).** If the landlord doesn't back off and you need to press the matter in court, you may need this letter as proof that you've complained of the behavior. And if the landlord agrees to a reasonable plan covering times and reasons for entry, reduce that understanding to a letter, too.

- **Never go away for extended periods of time without notifying the landlord.** Some states give landlords the right to enter if they discover you're not around. To avoid the possibility that the landlord will enter to check up, alert her of your plans and comply with reasonable requests such as turning off the heat in winter, draining the pipes, or securing the windows. If you take care of these matters, she'll have less need (or excuse) to come in.

- **Never withhold rent in response to your landlord's unauthorized entry.** Unfortunately, rent withholding is not the proper legal response to even the most obnoxious entry.

- **Never change the locks without the landlord's consent.** If your landlord is violating your privacy rights, your answer lies in the law (as in lawsuits and moving out), not locksmiths.

A. Entry by the Landlord

Your rental unit is your home and ought to be respected as such. About half the states have statutes (laws written by state legislators) specifying when and how landlords may legally enter rented property. (See "State Laws on Landlord's Access to Rental Property" in Appendix 2 for details.) In some states, your right to privacy may instead be the product of judge-made law and will be contained in court opinions issued by your state's appellate courts. And, in some states, you'll find that neither the legislators nor the judges have made law that protects the privacy rights of tenants. (In this event, your only hope is that your state constitution includes a broad right to privacy, which you can cite if you need to press the point with your landlord.)

If you find, after checking Appendix 2, that your state lacks a privacy statute, you'll have to research the case law or get help from a lawyer or tenants' rights group to find out how much privacy protection you can expect.

You can bargain for privacy protection if your state has no statute. During lease negotiations, simply ask the landlord to include a reasonable clause covering reasons for entry, amount of notice, and time of entry. A sample is provided below. Most landlords will be hard-pressed to say no to such a reasonable clause. If the landlord balks, it's a sure sign that he won't be reasonable in other respects, too. Continue on in your housing search!

SAMPLE PRIVACY CLAUSE

Clause _____. Entry by the Landlord. Landlord or his agent will not enter Tenant's home except to deal with an emergency; to make necessary or agreed repairs; to supply necessary or agreed services; or to show the unit to potential purchasers, tenants, or repair persons. Unless there is an emergency, Landlord will give Tenant at least 24 hours' written notice of the date, time, and purpose of the intended entry and will schedule entries during normal business hours, Monday-Friday.

---

1. Allowable Reasons to Enter

Landlords can always enter your rental unit under certain situations:

- **When you give permission.** There's nothing wrong with agreeing to a landlord's request to inspect for needed repairs. Many landlords schedule once- or twice-yearly walk-throughs to check for necessary maintenance. (You may see a provision establishing this practice in your lease or rental agreement.) Actually, most tenants are delighted when the landlord is so conscientious! But more frequent visits are generally unnecessary (unless there is a need to address a persistent problem, such as an insect infestation). Don't let yourself be coerced into "agreeing" to excessive visits that become harassing. These are illegal.

- **Any time there is a genuine emergency.** Common sense is the name of the game here: a broken dishwasher hardly qualifies, yet windows left wide open in the face of a driving rainstorm would.

- **To make needed repairs or improvements.** Most states allow the landlord to enter to perform his maintenance duties. This includes entry with contractors or designers as well as workmen. Your landlord must still give proper notice and enter at reasonable hours, as explained below.

- **To show property to prospective tenants or purchasers.** If you've given notice or your lease is about to expire, you must accommodate your landlord's reasonable efforts to rerent. The same is true when he attempts to sell the building or refinance. However, you are not obligated to hold endless open houses or accommodate showings with insufficient notice. Losing the use of your home every Saturday morning for an open house or being expected to clear out while potential buyers tramp through two or three times a week would be unreasonable in most people's estimation.

Ask for a reduction in rent in exchange for short notice or frequent showings to prospective tenants or buyers. After all, you are hardly getting what you've paid for (a quiet, undisturbed home) with strangers constantly waltzing through. A smart landlord will realize that your gracious cooperation is well worth a few dollars less each month.

Never put up with a lock-box. These are metal boxes affixed to the front door that hold a key to your home and can be opened by anyone knowing the code—typically, local real estate agents. It enables them to enter without notice and at any time, completely circumventing any state law on tenant privacy. Say "No," and if the owner or agent objects, write a letter to the real estate agent's main office with a copy to your state's real estate licensing board.

- **When the landlord believes you have abandoned the property.** If your landlord thinks you've skipped out without giving any notice or returning the key, he may legally enter. For example, if a neighbor reports seeing a moving van drive away and the utilities have been shut off, it's reasonable to conclude that you've left for good. Some states allow landlords to enter when you have left for an extended period of time, in order to perform needed or preventative maintenance.

"QUIET ENJOYMENT" IS NOT A SEDATE PARTY

Every landlord is bound by a legal principle known as the "covenant of quiet enjoyment." This archaic-sounding bit of legalese actually packs quite a punch: It's your right to be left in peace, free of your landlord's illegal intrusions. Especially in states that do not have specific access statutes, this age-old principle can come in handy if your landlord persists in unlawful entries that significantly interfere with your right to kick back, relax, and not worry about who's coming in the door unannounced. You may need to rely on it if the landlord refuses to back off. (See Section D, below.)

2. You're Entitled to Fair Warning

Most state access laws require landlords to give you 24 hours' to two days' notice before entering your rental unit in nonemergency situations. A few states simply require landlords to provide "reasonable" notice. (See "State Laws on Landlords' Access to Rental Property" in Appendix 2.)

If your state requires your landlord to give you only "reasonable" notice, you'll want to know how this translates into hours and days. Twenty-four hours is about right. In some circumstances, less notice (say, ten or 15 hours) might be fine—for example, think twice about objecting if your landlord finds out Thursday evening that an electrician is available Friday morning to install the extra outlets that you requested. Except for an emergency, less than four hours' notice is not ordinarily considered reasonable.

3. Any Old Time?

Most state access laws either do not specify what hours a landlord may enter your rental unit or simply allow entry at "reasonable times." Weekdays between 9 a.m. and 6 p.m. would seem to be reasonable times, and perhaps Saturdays between 10 a.m. and 1 p.m. Some states specify "normal business hours," which leaves it open as to whether Saturday would be a reasonable time.

STANDING ON YOUR HIGH HORSE IS RISKY

Common sense suggests that if your landlord does not have a history of invading your privacy, you're better off accommodating requests for entry, especially if the purpose is to make repairs that will benefit you. Objecting to legal entries without solid reasons may result in:

- **An eviction.** As long as your landlord complies with your state law as to reasons for entry and notice periods, your refusal to allow access can result in an eviction lawsuit.

- **A termination at the end of the month or a nonrenewal at the end of the lease.** If your landlord concludes you are too difficult to deal with, he may simply give you a 30-day notice or not renew the lease rather than put up with you.

- **A difficult working relationship.** Don't expect much help or understanding when you make repair requests or float an occasional plea to pay the rent late. Landlords have long memories.

This is not to say that you should surrender your rights to privacy out of craven fear. By no means should you. But don't be hard-nosed just for the principle involved.

B. Entry by Others

Your landlord is not the only one who may enter your rental unit. This section describes situations when other people such as municipal inspectors may want entry to your home.

1. Health, Safety, or Building Inspections

While your state may give you significant protections against entry by your landlord, the rules are different when it comes to entry by state or local health, safety, or building inspectors. Generally, inspectors may enter when they have reliable information, such as a complaint from a credible neighbor, that there's a health or safety problem inside. If you refuse entry, usually they'll return with a warrant and sometimes a police officer who will make sure that you don't prevent access.

Many cities now run random multidwelling inspections, designed to catch building and health code violations before tenants complain. You are entitled to reasonable notice (many ordinances have specified notice periods). Again, your refusal to allow the inspectors to enter will simply delay the inevitable.

2. The Cops

If the police have a valid search or arrest warrant, you have to let them in. The "notice" period is rather short—about as long as it takes them to knock and announce their presence! In addition, they can enter with no notice at all (forcibly if necessary) in order to interrupt a crime, apprehend a fleeing suspect, prevent the imminent destruction of evidence, or prevent a catastrophe such as a fire.

⚠️ **Don't expect your landlord to let your friends in.** Aside from the situations explained above, your landlord has no authority to allow anyone into your home without your consent. If your landlord lets in someone who purports to be your long-lost auntie but turns out to be a creative burglar, the landlord will be liable. Landlords who understand the risk they are taking are naturally unwilling to open tenants' doors for others.

C. Limits on Your Guests

Some landlords limit guests' visits—for example, no more than ten days in any six-month period—to avoid having a guest turn into an unauthorized new tenant. (See Chapter 1 for an explanation of the landlord's right to screen and approve occupants.) A few overly concerned landlords go overboard by keeping tabs on legitimate guests who stay overnight or for a few days.

Some leases, rental agreements, or rules and regulations will require you to register any overnight guest. As you probably would suspect, it's overkill to require you to inform your landlord of a guest who will stay only a day or two. Extreme behavior in this area—whether by an owner or a management employee—can be considered an invasion of privacy for which you may sue in small claims court if gentle persuasion fails.

MORE LANDLORD MUZZLES

Your landlord should refrain from:

- **Giving information about you to strangers who have no legitimate need to know.** This means that your landlord may give information about your creditworthiness or stability to prospective landlords, employers, banks, or creditors, but only if the question is directly related to a legitimate business need, such as your request for credit or a loan. Cautious landlords will ask you for a signed release before they answer even legitimate questions, but legally they are not required to have a release as long as the questions are legit.

- **Bothering you at work.** While you want your landlord to have your work phone number in case of an emergency, you don't want calls unless it's absolutely necessary. If you get persistent and embarrassing calls, write a tough letter demanding that they stop. If as the result of the landlord's conduct you lose your job or a promotion, see a lawyer—you may have the makings of a worthwhile lawsuit.

- **Spying on you.** Nosy interrogations and surveillance can give you reason to sue a landlord for invasion of privacy.

- **Neat tricks like turning off the power or changing the locks.** In most states, no matter how far behind you may be in the rent, your landlord may not lock you out or turn off any utilities. Known as "self-help" evictions, these moves expose the landlord to significant liabilities. The only legal way to evict you is through an actual eviction lawsuit.

- **Sexual harassment.** Harassment of a sexual nature is a form of discrimination that is against the law in every state. If your landlord engages in persistent and serious, unwanted advances, see an attorney. If you fear for your safety, contact your local police department.

D. How to Get Your Landlord to Back Off

As you no doubt know too well, it's one thing to *have* a right, while it's sometimes quite another to enjoy that right. Alas, getting your nosy landlord to cool it may not be an easy task, especially if his intrusiveness is annoying but just this side of illegal. Still, there are proven methods that may, with persistence, get results.

1. Have a Chat

The first step is to simply have a conversation, as friendly as possible, and ask that the behavior stop. If there is anything redeeming in your landlord's actions—his unannounced entries are for the purpose of fixing something that really needs to be done, for example—be sure to acknowledge that you appreciate his good intentions. Then explain that it would *really* be great if he could give you reasonable notice and so on. Follow up with a letter of understanding. (See Chapter 2, Section G.) A sample is shown below.

FRIENDLY LETTER ASKING LANDLORD TO RESPECT TENANT'S PRIVACY

August 5, 200X

Frank Lee Nosee
123 Main St.
Portland, Oregon 33221

Dear Mr. Nosee:

Thanks for sending your plumber over yesterday to fix my bathtub leak. I really appreciate your prompt response. As I mentioned when we spoke in the hall, I would have preferred to be notified when the plumber was scheduled to come because my dog can sometimes be temperamental around strangers. Thanks for your promise to give me at least 24 hours' notice in the future so I can arrange to be home.

Sincerely,
Heywood U. Bachoff
Green Gables Apartment #4B
526 Grover Road
Portland, Oregon 33221
503-555-4567

2. Get Tough

If your friendly chat and confirming letter don't get results, it's time to get heavy. Write another letter, this time directing your landlord's attention to the legal consequences of her refusal to respect your rights. Be sure you've done your homework first, by checking to see whether your state has a statute that covers tenant privacy or, failing that, whether there are court decisions upholding your rights.

These letters are not just exercises in futility—if you decide to press on and sue or utilize another significant remedy, you'll need evidence that you *first* brought the problem to the landlord's attention and did all that a reasonable person could do to persuade her to shape up. Be sure to keep a copy of your letter (and all landlord communications) in a safe place, and send the letter return-receipt requested. Another sample is shown below.

GET TOUGH LETTER ASKING LANDLORD TO RESPECT TENANT'S PRIVACY

September 19, 200X

I. Sellum Real Estate Co.
11 Peach Street
Cleveland, Ohio 77665

Dear Mr. Sellum:

Several times in the last two months your resident manager, Pete Tuttle, has entered my apartment when I was not at home and without notifying me in advance. Following the second such visit, I wrote to you on August 20, demanding that these unannounced entries stop at once.

In spite of my letter, Pete continued to enter when I was not home and without notice. One time when I was home sick from work, he simply walked in without knocking.

None of these entries involved an emergency—in fact, there was no real purpose for these visits. These intrusions have caused me considerable anxiety and stress, to the point that my peaceful enjoyment of my tenancy has been seriously disrupted.

This letter is to formally notify you that I value my privacy highly and insist that my legal rights to that privacy, as guaranteed to me under Ohio Rev. Code Ann. Sec. 5321.04(B) & 5321.05(B), be respected. Specifically, in nonemergency situations, I am entitled to 24 hours' notice of your (or your employee's) intent to enter my home, plus a clearly stated purpose of the entry.

I assume this letter will be sufficient to correct this matter. If you want to talk about this, please call me at home (555-7890) at night before 10 p.m.

Yours truly,
Ivanna Favor
789 Porter Street, #3
Cleveland, Ohio 77665
216-555-7890

⚠ **Never change the locks without permission.** Many state statutes expressly forbid tenants from doing so. Violating the law may result in the termination of your tenancy. And if your lease or rental agreement forbids you from altering the premises without the landlord's okay, the installation of a new lock will trigger this clause—again with the risk that your tenancy will be terminated.

3. Sue Your Landlord

If your words and letters get nowhere, it's time to see a lawyer or head for small claims court. Depending on the circumstances, you may be able to sue your landlord for:

- trespass: entering your rental space without consent or proper authority
- invasion of privacy: interfering with your right to be left alone
- breach of implied covenant of quiet enjoyment: interfering with your right to the undisturbed use of your home (see Section A, above)
- intentional infliction of emotional distress: a pattern of illegal acts by someone (in this case, the landlord or manager) who intended to and did cause serious emotional consequences to you.

Be forewarned that it may be hard to prove much in the way of money damages if the intrusions are annoying but not extreme. Most likely, a judge will figure that you have not been harmed much if, on one occasion, your landlord merely walked on your rug and opened and closed your door, and you won't be awarded much money for compensation.

However, if you can show a repeated pattern of illegal entry and the fact that you asked the landlord to stop it, or even one clear example of outrageous conduct, you may be able to get a substantial recovery. You'll probably want an attorney for this kind of case, especially if you bring your case in a court other than small claims court.

4. Move Out

Repeated abuses of your right to privacy may justify your breaking the lease and moving out, without liability for future rent. Some state statutes even include this as an available remedy.

If your statute doesn't explicitly give you the option of leaving when the landlord violates the privacy laws, or if you don't even have the protection of a privacy statute, don't despair. There's still a way to leave legally. Your legal theory is that the landlord's actions violated the "implied covenant of quiet enjoyment." (See Section A, above.) Since that covenant, or promise, is automatically present in every rental situation, your landlord has broken the lease. That breach leaves you free to leave.

It's a good idea to try mediation before packing up and moving out or heading for court. In fact, in many small claims courts you'll be sent to mediation before your case will be heard by a judge, so you might as well do it yourself early on. (Mediation is explained in more detail in Chapter 13, Section B.)

RULES TO RENT BY

You can go a long way toward ensuring your rights to privacy by following these tips:

- **Learn your state's law on tenant privacy,** particularly the permissible reasons for landlord entry and the amount of notice required.
- **Bargain for an access clause in your lease or rental agreement** if you aren't protected by a state statute or court decision.
- **Contact the owner if it's the manager or supe who's giving you a bad time.** Often, the owners don't know what their employees are doing.
- **Speak with other tenants to learn whether they, too, are the unhappy recipients of nosy intrusions.** If many complain, more attention is given.
- **Suggest mediation before filing suit or moving out.** Community-based landlord-tenant mediation services may help.

Chapter 9

How Tenancies Change and End

Sooner or later, you'll move on. Although not as complicated as the application and move-in process, moving out does involve more than dropping the keys on the manager's desk and waving goodbye as your U-Haul pulls away. You need to think about:

- how much advance notice you must give to end a month-to-month tenancy
- what happens if you *don't* give the required notice
- what can happen if you give notice and then don't leave
- what are your options if you want to get out of a lease, and
- what to do to make sure you get your deposit back.

TENANT TRAPS

Read this chapter to find out why you should:

- **Never leave without giving legal notice.** You'll be liable for at least a month's rent (if you have a rental agreement) and perhaps several months' rent (if you have a lot of time remaining on a lease). At the very least, you can kiss your deposit goodbye.
- **Never stay on after your lease has expired without signing a new rental document.** You may think that your lease self-renews, but in most states it doesn't, it simply changes to a month-to-month tenancy. This puts you in a precarious position if you want to stay for a while.
- **Never prepare to move without understanding your landlord's rules for cleaning up and getting them in writing.** Not only will you not know what's required, but your landlord will have a golden opportunity to change the standards *after* you've done all the work.
- **Never expect the landlord to use the security deposit for the last month's rent unless he agrees.** In some states, there are significant penalties for this ploy.

A. Changing Your Tenancy Without Ending It

Once you sign a lease or rental agreement, it's a legal contract between you and your landlord. Every understanding in it is binding for the life of the agreement: one month for month-to-month rental agreements and the term of the lease for leases.

So how can you or your landlord makes changes in the lease or rental agreement? The rules are different for leases and rental agreements. And if the proposed change is something you both agree to, there are yet different rules, as we'll explain below.

1. Changes in Month-to-Month Rental Agreements

If you rent month to month, chances are you'll see at least one change during your time at this address: a rent hike. Your landlord may also decide on other changes, such as the amount of the security deposit or whether to allow pets. You, too, may be able to negotiate your way towards more favorable terms—like the parking spot you've wanted for months. How you or your landlord may accomplish these changes depends on whether you both agree to the change. Here's how it works.

a. Changes That You Both Agree Upon

Since your rental agreement is a binding contract for its one-month life, neither you nor the landlord may unilaterally decide that there will be immediate changes, such as a rent hike or the removal of a guaranteed parking spot. If the landlord wants to impose these new understandings and you object, he'll have to follow the notice rules, as explained below in Subsection b. And if you feel that you cannot continue living there unless the landlord makes changes in your favor, you too will need to follow the notice rules that will allow you to leave if the landlord won't play ball.

However, there is nothing to stop you and the landlord from agreeing at any time to any changes the two of you both wish. To make immediate changes in a rental agreement, simply write the changes into the original document and make sure both of you sign and date the change. Or if the rental agreement is saved in electronic format, the landlord can simply enter the changes into the electronic document and print out a new agreement, ready for signatures.

b.   Changes Proposed by the Landlord

Landlords and tenants sometimes agree on rental agreement changes, but it's more common for landlords to announce unwelcome news such as rent increases, a decrease in services, or a variation on a common area rule. Your landlord doesn't need your consent when he announces a change in your rental agreement—but he doesn't get to impose it immediately, either. All that's required is that he give you the legal notice period: 30 days in most states.

Assuming you stay, you don't have to redo the entire rental agreement. The landlord can cross out the old language, write in the new, and initial and date the changes (he'll probably ask you to initial it, too). Or, he may add an addendum page. If the change is significant and the landlord has the agreement on a computer, he may choose to print out a new agreement, incorporating the change.

What can you do if you don't like the landlord's proposed change? If you can't talk him out of it, you can walk. Remember, though, you'll still need to give legal notice to end your tenancy, which is usually the same length of time as the notice period to change its terms (30 days, typically). If you give notice of your intention to leave on the same day you get notice about the landlord's change, you'll be legally free to leave before the change takes effect. However, if you wait a period of time before giving notice, the changes will take effect before your obligations as a tenant end. (See Section B, below, on ending a tenancy.)

c. Changes Proposed by the Tenant

Tenants, too, can propose changes in a rental agreement, such as asking
for permission to bring in an additional roommate. If the landlord agrees,
great—follow the advice in Subsection a, above. In most situations,
however, you have very little bargaining power if the landlord balks.
Your best ally when pressing for better terms is your track record as a
stable, good tenant. If the landlord is smart, he'll take steps to retain
you as a tenant by keeping you happy. (See Section A2c, below, for tips
on convincing the landlord.) If you don't prevail and it's an all-important
issue, your only alternative is to give your own termination notice, as
explained below in Section B2.

2. Changes in Leases

One of the advantages of having a lease is knowing that its terms are set
until it runs out. But there are ways to modify leases, as explained below.

a. Changes That You Both Agree Upon

The two of you are free to change the terms of your lease at any time if
you both want to. Follow the instructions for making changes in rental
agreements, above, in Subsection 1a.

b. Changes Proposed by the Landlord

Knowing that leases can't be changed except by mutual consent makes
some landlords nervous. Predictably, they want to be able to raise the
rent midlease, or they anticipate that they may want to make other
changes (such as decreasing services) that they aren't intent on imposing
at the start of the tenancy.

Landlords give themselves some flexibility by *writing the change into the lease itself.* You can think of it as a kind of option—to the landlord's benefit! For example, you may see a clause that specifies that the landlord "reserves the right to increase the rent by $50 at the end of six months." As long as the proposed change is certain as to time and amount (or other specific factors), you'll be bound by it if the landlord decides to impose it.

Watch out, however, for open-ended change rights, such as a clause giving the landlord the right to "raise the rent at any time." A court would probably not enforce a lease clause that is so vague. If you encounter a landlord who presents you with such a slippery clause, think carefully about doing business with him.

⚠️ **Some landlords use a lease clause giving them the right to make insubstantial changes during your lease.** Some states, as well, have statutes giving landlords the right to make small changes midlease. Naturally, there is often great debate over the meaning of an "insignificant" change. There will be little argument about truly minor changes (keeping the pool open an hour less on weekdays, for example) or obviously major ones (an increase in rent), but the situations that fall into the middle will invariably cause trouble. As a rule of thumb, if an issue is important enough to be included in a written lease in the first place (such as the provision of a parking spot), it's hard to imagine how it could also be classed as "inessential."

c.   Changes Proposed by the Tenant

Just as the landlord can't tinker with the lease terms while the lease is still in effect, neither can you. The landlord is entitled to hold you to your bargain, just as you can with respect to him. This doesn't mean, however, that you can't try some creative negotiating, as suggested below.

To convince your landlord to change the terms of a rental agreement or a lease midterm, show him that the change is:

- not a burden—it's a small matter to him but an important one to you, such as allowing you to bring in a roommate. Of course, your pal must have the same good-tenant qualifications that you did, and your place must be big enough to accommodate one more. (See Chapter 6 for more on bringing in a roommate.)

- actually a benefit—such as your request to set up a home business. After you point out the security advantages of having someone consistently at home during the weekdays, able to spot suspicious or dangerous conditions, your landlord might like the idea.

- necessary to enable you to stay—for example, if you've just inherited your best friend's pooch while she studies abroad, you'll have to move to a place that allows pets unless your landlord will bend his no-pets policy. This will only work if you're the kind of tenant the landlord wants to keep.

- something the landlord ought to do anyway—for instance, give you a nearby parking spot for the two months you'll be on crutches with a broken leg. While you could probably press for this accommodation by complaining to a fair housing agency or a judge (the rights of the disabled are explained in Chapter 5), you would certainly rather do it informally. For best results, don't threaten, just explain the strength of your position and the wisdom of doing things your way.

B. How Month-to-Month Tenancies End

A month-to-month tenancy renews (sometimes termed "rolls over") every 30 days. This means that if no one says anything about leaving, you can theoretically stay forever. But if your landlord wants you out, do you get any advance warning? And what are your obligations if *you* decide to pack up?

1. When Your Landlord Wants You Out

It's easy for a landlord to end a month-to-month tenancy. In most situations, he needn't give a reason (though acting on discriminatory or retaliatory motives is illegal; see Chapters 5 and 11). Except in New Hampshire, New Jersey, and most rent-controlled cities, where a legally recognized reason ("just cause") is required for terminations, landlords can give you the boot just because they feel like it.

Landlords must, however, give you fair warning. Thirty days is typical. Unless the rental agreement specifies otherwise, notice needn't be delivered on the day rent is due. If notice is given midterm, then your tenancy will run out in the middle of the next month.

All states, and even some cities (typically those with rent control), have their own very detailed rules and procedures for how landlords must prepare and serve termination notices. For example, some states specify that the notice be printed in a certain size or style of typeface. If your landlord doesn't follow these procedures, the notice terminating your tenancy may be invalid. But once you point out the mistake, either informally or as a legal defense to an eviction lawsuit, your landlord will probably simply correct his mistake and do it right the next time. If you want information on your state's exact requirements, consult your state statutes. (See "Landlord-Tenant Statutes" in Appendix 2.) Your state consumer protection agency or local tenants' rights organization may also have useful advice.

⚠ **If you receive a termination notice in the mail, which may be legal if the landlord couldn't deliver it to you personally, don't assume that you can add a few days to make up for the time in transit.** For example, a notice to terminate in 30 days that was mailed on the first but delivered by the mail carrier on the fifth may still be effective on the first of the next month, in spite of the fact that you have really received only 25, not 30, days, notice. Check your state statutes to find out for sure.

If your landlord attempts to terminate your tenancy without giving proper notice, you may decide to stay, wait for the eviction lawsuit to be filed against you, and fight it with the defense that the notice was defective. If the notice is truly defective, you'll probably survive the eviction, but the landlord will simply do it right the next time. Your gain: a few additional weeks at your old place. Your loss: time and effort spent in court, plus an eviction mark on your credit report, even though you won. You do the math.

Landlords hate courtrooms. If you need a few extra days, or even a month or two before moving, ask the landlord to extend your tenancy. In exchange, promise to go quietly at the appointed time. From the landlord's point of view, unless you're a troublemaker or he desperately needs the unit for some other reason, it's far more efficient to strike a deal than go through the expense and hassle of going to court. Put your offer in writing, which will assure the landlord of your good intentions—but remember, it will be devastating evidence against you in court should you renege on your promise, requiring the landlord to file an eviction to get you out.

If your landlord claims you've violated the lease—such as by failing to pay the rent—he may move quickly to terminate and evict. Notice periods for these situations are often much shorter, usually three to five days to pay up or move. Sometimes, tenants don't have the option of paying the rent or correcting the violation—they must move or face an eviction lawsuit. Defending yourself against an eviction for an alleged lease violation isn't covered in this book.

2. When You Want to Leave

It's equally easy for you, too, to get out of a rental agreement. Just give the required amount of notice to your landlord. If you mail the notice, be sure to take into account the amount of time your notice will spend in transit. To be safe, assume that the time begins running when the landlord receives the notice, instead of when you mailed it—the landlord may be counting from the date of mailing and may have rerented the unit as of that date. Contact the landlord and make sure you both agree as to which day will be your last (take a look at your state statutes first).

Usually you can send in your termination midterm, as can your landlord. But check your rental agreement—some landlords, anxious to avoid the hassles of being left with partial months, insist that notice be given on the day rent is due so that tenants move out at the end of a full rental period. This means that if rent is due on the first but you decide on the second that you want to move, you'll have to wait until the start of the next month before giving notice. In other words, if your rental agreement requires you to give notice on the first day of the month, and you give notice on any other day, in the eyes if the law it hasn't been given until the first day of the next month and won't expire until one month after that.

⚠ Watch out for rental agreements that lengthen your notice period and shorten your landlord's. Some rental agreements establish a notice period for tenants that is longer than the one specified by state law for terminating a tenancy. Or, a landlord may attempt to shorten his own notice period. Both moves are designed to give the landlord more flexibility and you less. In some states, these agreements are valid. Check your state statute and, if the issue isn't addressed there, contact your state's consumer protection agency. Valid or not, be advised that a landlord who expects tenants to be bound by his last-minute decisions and short notice periods is probably one to avoid.

What happens if you give less than the required amount of notice? It's simple: You can leave, but you pay rent for that period, anyway. For example, if you suddenly move out of a month-to-month unit where 30 days' notice is required, the landlord will probably simply deduct from your security deposit the amount of rent you would have paid if you had delivered the required notice.

3. What If You Change Your Mind?

Notice is notice—there's no retraction period. Once you have delivered your termination notice, that's it. Your landlord is entitled to hold you to it and need not even listen to you as you attempt to explain why circumstances now make it impossible or unwise for you to move.

If you decide to stay put and hope that this business of moving will just blow over, think carefully. If your landlord has rented your place to someone else after you've given notice, but then you decide to stay on ("hold over"), there's the problem of the tenant who expected to take your place. You can be liable to this tenant for his temporary housing costs incurred while the landlord evicts you or while the disappointed tenant resumes his own housing search.

There's more. If the disappointed tenant walks away in disgust, your landlord will have a pile of rental expenses occasioned by your expected departure (advertisements, applicant screening costs, time spent showing your unit) that now appear to be a waste of her time and money. She'll have an easy time deducting these expenses from your security deposit and then suing you in small claims court if you don't replenish the deposit. In short, don't announce that you're leaving until you're really sure.

4. Bailing Out of a Bad Place

If your landlord seriously violates the rental agreement or fails to fulfill her legal responsibilities—for example, by not correcting serious health or safety problems—you may be able to move out legally without waiting for the clock to terminate your tenancy. You can leave with no written notice or by giving less notice than is otherwise required. Called a "constructive eviction," this doctrine typically applies only when living conditions are intolerable—for example, if you've had no heat for an extended period in the winter.

The conditions that will justify a constructive eviction vary slightly under the laws of different states. Generally, if the landlord is on notice that a rental unit has serious habitability problems for an extended time, you're entitled to move out on short notice or, in extreme cases, without giving notice. (See Chapter 7, which explains all of your options when faced with an unlivable unit, for more information.)

C. What Happens When Your Lease Runs Out

A lease lasts for a fixed term, typically one year, then simply ends of its own accord at the end of the term. Your landlord doesn't have to give you notice of the end of the lease, because you already know (or should remember!) that the time is up. At this point, you must either:

- move
- sign a new lease, with the same or different terms, or
- stay on as a month-to-month tenant *with your landlord's approval*. In most states, the terms and conditions of the old lease (such as no pets) will carry over into your new, oral month-to-month tenancy.

If you do none of these things and your landlord wants you to move on, you are considered a "holdover" tenant and will probably be evicted. The landlord can file an eviction lawsuit within a very few days, and you'll have little chance of winning unless you can show that the refusal to renew was illegal because it was discriminatory (see Chapter 5) or an act of retaliation (see Chapter 11). If your intent in staying on is to buy time, forget it—eviction lawsuits for holdovers are fast affairs. And if your lease has an "attorney fees" clause in it (see Chapter 2, Section C14), you'll be on the hook for your landlord's lawyer and court costs. Even if you capitulate on the courthouse steps, these costs will stick—as will the notation on your credit report that an eviction suit was filed against you. Far better to negotiate for a little more time, as suggested in Section B, above.

D. Breaking a Lease and Leaving Early

For all sorts of reasons—a job transfer, an invitation to move in with someone else, or deciding that you just don't like the place—you may want to leave before your lease ends. If you're lucky, your landlord will agree to let you go—a response most likely if your landlord is a decent sort or there is a shortage of rental housing and hordes of eager applicants—or, ironically, if the landlord considers you a pain in the neck and would be delighted to say good-bye. But what if you don't have your landlord's official *bon voyage?* Like lots of legal answers, it depends, mostly on your state law and the saturation of the rental market.

1. Most Landlords Must Rerent

Let's start with the basics: Your lease is a contract, obligating you to pay rent for the entire term. The fact that you pay in monthly installments doesn't change the fact that you owe the landlord for the entire amount. So if you split early, what's to stop the landlord from suing you for the remaining months' rent?

Fortunately, in most states landlords cannot simply sit back and wait for the term to end, then sue you for the months you weren't there. They must take reasonable steps to rerent the place and credit that rent to your debt. This duty goes by a mouthful of words—"the landlord's duty to mitigate damages." The chart "Landlords' Duty to Rerent the Premises" in Appendix 2 notes which states require landlords to mitigate. This tenant-friendly rule has some limitations, however:

- You may still be responsible for the costs of advertising and showing the unit.
- Your landlord must take *reasonable* steps to rerent, not heroic ones. He needn't put your unit at the top of his list of properties to rent, and he doesn't have to offer it for a song.

- The landlord needn't accept any old applicant who walks in the door. He's entitled to be as choosy with the next tenant as he was with you.

Unfortunately, many landlords are unaware of their duty to rerent for the benefit of the departing tenant. And even if they are aware of the rule, the notion that they must make an effort to minimize the financial hit to someone who broke their lease is often tough for them to swallow. Their response is to keep the security deposit at least and often to send a threatening letter demanding the balance of the rent. If this sounds like what happened to you, read on.

2. When Your Landlord Hasn't Hustled for a New Tenant

If you've broken your lease and taken off, expect to lose a month's rent even if state law requires your landlord to mitigate—most judges will give the landlord a month of rent as damages, no matter how quickly the landlord advertised and showed the unit—or how quickly he *could* have rented it if he had tried. Your landlord will take this month's rent out of your security deposit.

But being asked to pony up the rest of the rent due under your lease is something else entirely. If your landlord sends you a righteous letter demanding the balance due under your lease, a polite letter, citing your state's law, might disabuse the landlord of his "right" to sit idle and collect on an empty apartment. The sample letter below shows how one tenant has done this. With luck, your landlord will back off.

But what if your letter doesn't produce the desired result? If you are sued for an enormous amount of rent or have a sizeable deposit sitting in the landlord's bank account, you'll be headed for court—either as a defendant if the landlord sues you, or as a plaintiff if you sue to recover some of your deposit.

SAMPLE LETTER ALERTING LANDLORD TO THE DUTY TO MITIGATE

June 21, 200X

Bill C. Lecter
90 Maple Avenue
Monroe, CA 90000

Dear Mr. Lecter:

Until recently, I rented your flat at 78 Oak Street in Monroe. Unfortunately, a job transfer made it necessary for me to move to Harding, some 100 miles away. As I explained in late May, I had no choice but to break my year's lease on June 1, 200X. The lease had six months left. I left owing no rent for the time that I lived there.

I was disappointed to receive your letter dated June 18, 200X, in which you informed me that you expect me to pay you for the remaining six months' rent. You stated that you will keep my entire security deposit (two months' rent) and have demanded that I pay you for the remaining four months.

May I direct your attention to California Civil Code Section 1951.2, which requires a landlord to use reasonable efforts to rerent after a tenant has broken the lease. As you know, rentals are scarce in this town, and I would think that you could rerent my flat, which is quite nice, fairly quickly. While I am prepared to cover one month while you prepare, advertise, and show the unit, I am certainly not willing to pay further rent on an apartment that you have purposefully left empty.

Please reimburse me for the one month's rent that you withheld from my deposit.

Yours truly,
Tom Tenant
23 Seventh Avenue
Harding, CA 90000
626-555-4567

If the courthouse is on the horizon, you'll have to have some proof that the landlord failed to mitigate. Be smart and, after you leave, collect evidence of the landlord's efforts in the rerental department (or ask a friend in the area to do so). Find out whether the landlord advertised (check the rental ads for a month or so), showed the unit (ask the neighbors), rented comparable units but not yours, or in fact rented the unit and is now attempting to double-dip. In some states, if you end up in court arguing that the landlord failed to take steps to rerent, you can't sit back and wait for the landlord to produce proof that he diligently tried to rerent. Instead, *you* will have to supply the proof of his laziness.

Offer your landlord a replacement tenant. If you can find a sub who is likely to pass your landlord's screening criteria, offer that tenant when (or before) you break the lease. Ideally, the landlord will accept the sub (you've really saved him a lot of time and hassles), and you, too, will end up not being liable for any unrented months. In addition, if the landlord unreasonably refuses an acceptable would-be tenant, he'll have a hard time arguing in court that he took reasonable efforts to find a replacement.

RULES TO RENT BY

- **Understand how much notice (advance warning) your landlord must give you before terminating or changing your rental agreement.** Know how much notice you, too, must give before moving out.
- **Insist that important changes to leases or rental agreements be reduced to writing, and signed by you and the landlord.**
- **If you need to break a lease and move early, try to find a replacement tenant who has the same good credit and rental history that you did (or better).**

Chapter 10

Getting Your Deposit Back

It's a rare departing tenant who doesn't have some hassle with the landlord over the return of the deposit. Some landlords don't know the law, and many haven't set up their business to make it clear from the outset what they expect, in the way of cleanliness, when their tenants move out. You can do a lot both to educate the landlord and to impose some standards that you can count on.

Inspect and photograph the rental unit before you move in. Without objective proof of the condition of the unit when you moved in, it will be difficult to effectively counter a landlord's claim that you caused damage that, in fact, was there when you took over. Pictures don't lie. (See our move-in tips in Chapter 2, Section C.)

A. How Your Landlord May Use Your Deposit

Legally, a landlord may use the deposit for any cleaning or repairs necessary to restore the rental unit to its condition at the beginning of the tenancy (minus ordinary wear and tear), and to cover unpaid back rent (and a reasonable amount of future rent if you break a lease and leave early). We emphasize that the landlord may not use your security deposit for the cost of remedying the results of ordinary use. This means that if the paint is ruined because your toddler mistook the wall for an easel, expect to be charged; but if the carpet needs to be replaced because it's ten years old and is simply worn out, it's the landlord's responsibility.

Unfortunately, it's not always easy to decide what constitutes ordinary wear and tear or what must be done to leave a rental unit clean. Here are some guidelines:

- You shouldn't be charged for damage or filth that was there when you moved in.
- If the landlord can repair an item without diminishing its function or appearance, he ought to choose that over replacement.

- The longer you've lived in a place, the greater the amount of wear and tear.
- If you've paid a nonrefundable cleaning fee (some states allow them in addition to security deposits), you shouldn't be charged for additional cleaning.

THE FINAL BLOW TO WORN FURNISHINGS

Red wine on a brand-new white carpet? Face it, you'll pay for this one. But what about stains on an old, worn carpet; or scratches from your dog's paws on a floor already marred by water damage; or major nail holes on a wall that hasn't been painted in years? Should you be expected to pay the full cost for refurbishing these worn, yet still-usable items, simply because your error was the last straw?

Of course not. Still, many a landlord will try to stick a tenant with the entire bill because the tenant's goof prematurely ended the life of the carpet, floor, or paint job. Unfortunately, there is practically no clear law on the subject. You caused the early demise of the rug, floor, or wall, but how much should you fairly pay?

The answer begins by remembering that normal wear and tear must be covered by the landlord, which means that replacement costs of worn-out items are borne by him, too. So, suppose that the carpet with a stain the size of New Hampshire originally cost $1,000 and had an expected life of ten years (normal wear and tear). At the end of these ten years, the carpet would be worth $0 (its value decreases by $100 per year), and the landlord would have to shell out the money to replace it. If your mishap occurs in the fifth year, your landlord will lose $500 worth of use. Arguably, you owe him that amount.

This method of calculating damage costs is not accepted by everyone. And it is subject to some very big variables. For example, the useful life of a carpet in the home of a fastidious single tenant will be longer than the life of the same carpet used by a family of four. Nevertheless, it's one way to approach being charged for the entire amount. If you use this method, be sure to collect information on the "useful life" of the item you're being charged for and its original cost. If you go to small claims court to argue for the return of your deposit, you'll need this proof.

B. The Mechanics of Getting the Deposit Back

Depending on the state, landlords generally have from 14 to 30 days after you leave—whether voluntarily or by eviction—to return all or part of your deposit. (State laws are in Appendix 2.) The landlord must mail either of the following to your last known address (or forwarding address, if known):

- Your entire deposit, with interest if required (the chart in Appendix 2 lists state laws requiring interest).

- A written, itemized statement as to how the deposit has been applied toward back rent and costs of cleaning and damage repair, together with whatever is left of the deposit, including any interest that is required. In most states, landlords must send the itemization along with any deposit balance. A few states add an additional step that gives tenants time to respond to proposed deductions before they are actually made.

If your landlord is slow in returning your deposit, a reminder letter is in order. (In some states, deliberate or "bad faith" retention of the deposit subjects the landlord to sizeable penalties.) Ask for the amount to be refunded, cite your state or local law regarding deposits, send the letter certified, and keep a copy. Known as a "demand letter," you'll need to show it to the judge if you end up in court attempting to collect your deposit.

SAMPLE LETTER DEMANDING RETURN OF SECURITY DEPOSIT

July 15, 200X

Sandy Beach
5 Lake View Drive
Washburn, Illinois 12345

Dear Ms. Beach:

As you know, until May 30, 200X, I rented Apartment #4 at
1492 Columbus Avenue. I gave 30 days' notice on May 1,
and moved out owing no rent. The apartment was not damaged
in any way.

As of today, I have received neither my $750 security deposit
nor any accounting from you for that money. Under Illinois law
(Ill. Rev. Stat. Ch. 765 para. 710, 715), I was entitled to receive
my deposit, including an itemization of any deductions, 30 days
after my tenancy ended—that is, by June 30, 2004. You are now
over two weeks late.

Please return the deposit to me immediately. If I do not receive
my money by July 25, I will regard your retention of my deposit
as showing bad faith and will sue you in small claims court for
$1,500, which is double the amount of my deposit as allowed
under Illinois law.

I look forward to receiving my deposit forthwith at the above
address.

Yours truly,

Andrew Noble
76 Noview Drive
Evans, Illinois 12345

C. Avoiding Fights Over Deposits

Most deposit hassles involve disputes over "How clean is clean?" or "What's wear and tear?" Disputes over back rent or replacements are more rare. Unfortunately, no statute or court opinion will give you a universally accepted standard for cleanliness or "normal" wear and tear. Smart landlords announce their own definitions, usually in a set of rules and regulations or in a letter that follows the receipt or sending of a termination notice. These are perfectly legal as long as they are reasonable. Examples include:

- floors washed, stripped, and waxed (broom-clean won't do)
- carpets professionally steam-cleaned (more than just a thorough vacuuming)
- windows and mirrors washed
- kitchen appliances emptied of food and cleaned
- all trash and personal belongings removed (don't expect the landlord to dispose of your cast-offs).

If your landlord hasn't clarified his expectations, take control and do it for him. When your departure date nears, send him a letter explaining what you intend to do to ensure the return of your entire deposit (there's a sample below). You'll be on solid footing if you set your goals to correspond the condition of the place when you moved in—after all, the law requires no more.

What's the advantage of this procedure? If you've stayed with us since Chapter 2, Section G, and you remember the value of a letter of understanding, you'll recognize how nicely you've just prepared your landlord. If he doesn't object in writing he'll be locked in, legally speaking, to your plans. Assuming your plans are fair and you do a decent job (you should take photos or video, or have a witness willing to testify about the condition of the unit when you left), it will be hard for the landlord to argue in court that you didn't do what he expected or did it poorly.

SAMPLE LETTER EXPLAINING TENANT'S CLEANING PLANS

May 15, 200X

Mr. Rusty Shaque
5 Leisure Lane
Lakeport, Illinois 60600

Dear Mr. Shaque,

As you know, I gave notice on April 30, 200X, that I intend to terminate my tenancy effective May 30, 200X. I intend to leave the apartment clean and undamaged, in the same condition it was in when I moved in a year ago, minus normal wear and tear. In particular, I intend to:

- vacuum all floors and carpets, and wax the hardwood floor in the kitchen
- wash bathroom floors and wall tiles
- clean all bathroom and kitchen appliances with cleaning products designed for these areas; clean oven and turn off and clean refrigerator
- cold-water wash the cotton drapes in the kitchen and bathroom
- vacuum drapes in living room and bedroom
- wash the interior surfaces of the windows
- remove all rubbish and personal items

I believe that thoroughly accomplishing these tasks will satisfy my obligations under Illinois law to leave my rental unit clean. And since my apartment has not been damaged and I owe no back rent, I expect a full and prompt refund of my $750 security deposit. Please let me know in writing within five days of your receipt of this letter if my cleaning plan is not acceptable to you. If I don't hear from you, I'll assume that you agree with it.

Yours truly,

P.T. Smart
11256 Seventh Avenue
Chicago, Illinois 60600

In most cases, your landlord will be so delighted that you intend to put some elbow grease into cleaning your unit that he wouldn't dream of objecting.

D. Suing to Get the Deposit Back

If your landlord has unfairly kept your deposit by making improper deductions or failing to return it within the time specified by your state's law, it's time to shift gears. You should send the landlord a letter (return receipt requested) asking for the return of your deposit or what you think your landlord owes you. In the letter, concisely review the main facts, ask for exactly what you want, and explain your legal rights. Conclude by stating that you will promptly sue in small claims court if necessary.

Hopefully, you've taken some of the suggestions throughout this chapter (such as nailing down what's expected in the way of cleaning and taking photos when you leave) so that you can head for court armed with helpful evidence. (For more information on small claims court, see Chapter 13, Section C.)

RULES TO RENT BY

- **Before you move out, find out exactly what the landlord expects in the way of cleaning.** If you get no answer, announce a cleaning plan of your own, designed to return the place to its condition (minus ordinary wear and tear) at the start of your tenancy. Unless the landlord objects, follow through with your plan.
- **Ask the landlord to inspect when you leave, and take your own photos.** You don't want to run the risk that you'll be charged for damage caused by the next tenant.
- **Be sure to write a demand letter before going off to court.**

Chapter 11

Landlord Retaliation

Rare is the tenant who, having asserted her rights, has not been rewarded with a landlord payback—whether in the form of petty harassment, a rent hike, or an all-out termination and eviction. The good news for most of you is that landlord retaliation is illegal in most states—landlords who engage in it can be stopped and sued, sometimes for big bucks. The bad news is that asserting your rights can be a hassle, involving court fights and lots of time. As much as it's possible, you'll do far better to choose your landlord wisely in the first place, as we advise in Chapter 1.

But suppose now that, despite your best efforts to live in a well-run building managed by businesspeople of integrity, your request for repairs has been met with the sudden loss of your parking spot; or your efforts to organize other tenants into complaining about security have earned you a termination notice. In this chapter, we'll explain what you can do about it.

TENANT TRAPS

Read this chapter to find out why you should:

- **Never be pushy without knowing whether your state will protect you if the landlord strikes back.** Some state laws do not, and some protect only certain actions. Without knowing your state's rules, you may come to regret your righteousness.
- **Never attempt to nail your landlord for illegal retaliation when there's a skeleton or two in your own closet.** Lots of information gets out in a legal fight, and you may open areas you wish had been left untouched.
- **Never go after your landlord without carefully weighing the pros and cons,** especially whether you would be better served by spending the time and energy looking for another place rather than inviting a legal battle.

A. Where Does the Law Protect You?

Everyone who has played in a school yard or worked with a jealous coworker understands the everyday meaning of retaliation: a nasty response to something you've done. Your action may have been on the edge itself (a shove on the basketball court that earns you an elbow in the face) or it may have been perfectly innocent (a job well done that shows up a colleague, who strikes back). Naturally, if you're wearing a white hat, you're in a better position to cry "Foul!"

The same rules apply when it comes to the legal meaning of retaliation. The laws of most states will protect you from landlord get-backs when you have acted within your tenant rights—in other words, you can expect legal protection if you are blameless and it's the landlord who began the shoving match. In almost all states, you cannot be retaliated against if you have:

- complained to a building inspector, fire department, health inspector, or other governmental agency about unsafe or illegal living conditions

- exercised your First Amendment rights to assemble and present your views collectively, as in joining or organizing a tenant union, or

- availed yourself of self-help strategies allowed by your state or local law, such as deducting money from the rent and using it to fix defects in the rental unit, or even withholding the rent entirely for an uninhabitable unit. (See Chapter 7.)

Only eight states—Alabama, Colorado, Georgia, Indiana, Oklahoma, Pennsylvania, South Dakota, and Wyoming—do not have statutes or court decisions protecting tenants against retaliation.

1. Differences in State Laws

It's important to understand that the antiretaliation laws will shield you
only for those activities that are mentioned in your state's statute. Not
all states protect tenants for all three types of actions mentioned above.
(Check your state's range by referring to "State Laws Prohibiting Landlord
Retaliation" in Appendix 2.) For example, in Washington, D.C., a tenant
who circulates a petition demanding better services cannot be retaliated
against; but that same activity would not be protected in Florida, since
"exercise of a legal right" isn't included in Florida's statute.

2. Don't Stretch Your Luck

Don't think that you can abuse the system and still avoid your landlord's
wrath. You must exercise your legal rights in good faith in order to be
protected. If you withhold rent with no valid reason; circulate a patently
scurrilous petition about your landlord; or file endless, groundless complaints with government agencies, no judge will prevent a landlord from
taking appropriate action (such as not renewing your lease or terminating
your rental agreement).

3. You Don't Have to Be Perfect

An honest mistake made during an otherwise valid attempt to exercise
your rights usually won't deprive you of the protection of your state's
antiretaliation statute. For example, suppose that in response to a broken
heater in the winter you withhold rent without complying strictly with
your state's notice requirement. Your angry landlord is likely to call you
on your error and demand the rent. If you pay it, can he then terminate
your tenancy? Assuming that the heater was truly broken and your mistake relatively minor, you'll be in a good position to argue that you still
deserve the benefit of your state law. Of course, you'd be far better off to
follow the withholding rules carefully, as we counsel in Chapter 7.

B. What Is Retaliation?

Now that you know what *you* can do, let's turn to what your landlord *cannot* do. The kinds of retaliatory acts covered by state statutes include:

- terminating a month-to-month tenancy or refusing to renew a lease, and following up with an eviction lawsuit if you decide to stay and fight
- increasing the rent, and
- decreasing services, such as locking the laundry room, draining the pool, removing cable access, or canceling the security service or doorman.

Of course, few landlords are dumb enough to announce a retaliatory plan. Chances are that they will cloak their real motives in a cover-up, such as the sudden need to rent to a long-lost aunt or their financial inability to keep up with the just-decreased service. It's up to you to expose the truth, as explained below in Section D.

C. Responding to Retaliation

If you're the object of your landlord's nasty moves, two responses are possible, depending on what the landlord has done:

- If the retaliation consists of a termination and eviction, you may want to stay and fight, defending yourself against eviction by proving to the judge that the real reason for the termination was illegal.
- If the retaliation is a rent hike, a reduction in services, or any other negative treatment, you may want to take the offensive by filing suit in small claims court. In your suit, you'd ask the judge to prohibit the rent hike, order the services reinstated (or a rent reduction to compensate you for the loss), or take other appropriate measures.

Sometimes you'll have a choice. For example, if the retaliation consists of a rent increase, you could refuse to pay and force the landlord to terminate and evict, banking on your antiretaliation statute as your defense. Or, you could immediately file suit in small claims court as soon as you get notice of the increase, hoping to resolve the issue before the increase kicks in. We strongly advise choosing the latter course whenever possible—if you lose, you can leave on your own terms, when and if you want to, without an eviction lawsuit going onto your credit report. On the other hand, if you force an eviction lawsuit your credit report will include this fact. Even if you win, this is not good news for any prospective landlord or employer.

By far the most common kind of retaliation, however, is of the petty sort. Before filing papers in small claims court, ask yourself if the issue is really worth your time and money to fight. And, unfortunately, many intensely annoying ploys are just not that big a deal to a judge, either.

IS THE RETALIATION A BIG DEAL?

If you think a rent hike or other negative treatment is motivated by your assertion of a tenant's legal right, you may decide to fight back. But before you do, ask yourself the following questions:

- **Are you covered?** Check your state statutes to make sure that you have antiretaliation protection for what you've done.
- **How soon after your action did the rent increase or negative treatment come?** Obviously, the shorter the interval between your exercise of a legal right and the date of the increase, the more suspicious it becomes.
- **How large was the increase; how onerous was the mean move?** Judges are more likely to view a large rent increase (rather than a small one) as the landlord's way to punish or drive away a troublesome tenant. Ditto with reductions in services.
- **Does the rent increase or nasty move affect you alone, or does it apply to many others?** Your chances of proving a retaliatory motive will be greatly increased if you can show that you alone, but not tenants in similar units, received the negative treatment.

- **Is your landlord known for repeatedly and seriously trampling on tenants' rights?** Your landlord's reputation is certainly a relevant factor if you contemplate challenging a rent increase. You can learn whether the landlord is a frequent visitor to landlord-tenant or small claims court by asking the local tenants' organization or even your fellow tenants. The judge may tell you that this information is irrelevant and won't be considered—but you may want to share it anyway, then listen politely while the judge gives you a little lecture on the rules of evidence.

- **How disruptive or expensive, from the landlord's point of view, was your exercise of a legal right?** It's easier to win the cases in which you can convince a judge that the landlord has a strong motive to get even. Did you cause the landlord considerable time, expense, aggravation, or embarrassment? For example, if you complained to the local health department that your housing is uninhabitable because the roof leaked, and the department ordered your landlord to put on a new roof, that's an expensive job that your landlord might resent highly. This anger could well prompt a retaliatory rent hike, you'll claim. Similarly, an accusation of discrimination against your landlord, even if he ultimately defeats it, could easily generate strong feelings of bitterness and retaliation. On the other hand, your isolated request for a necessary and inexpensive repair is far less likely in the eyes of a judge to motivate serious landlord revenge.

D. Proving That It's Retaliation

If you're determined to fight back by filing suit or hunkering down and defending against an eviction, there's one more issue you need to think about. How do you prove your landlord is trying to retaliate against you? In the real world, landlords are rarely so foolish as to say directly, "If you complain to the housing department, I'll evict you!" Instead, they're likely to stick it to you for a trumped-up reason, hoping to mask the fact that the real motive is to get rid of a tenant whom they regard as a troublemaker. Common examples of cover-ups that are really retaliations are:

- an unexplained termination that follows hard on the heels of a long-term tenant's legitimate decision to withhold the rent
- a refusal to renegotiate a lease following a tenant's complaint to the health department, and
- sending a termination notice alleging misuse of common facilities after a tenant has used the common room to bring tenants together to fight a proposed rent increase.

Fortunately, however, many states give tenants an edge when it comes to unmasking illegal reasons to end a tenancy. In 15 states, the landlord is presumed to be retaliating against you if a tenancy is ended (or services decreased) within a certain amount of time after your exercise of a legal right, typically six months but sometimes 90 days or one year. This means that it will be up to the landlord to prove to the judge, should you end up in court, that his motives were *not* retaliatory.

RULES TO RENT BY

- **Make sure you know what your state or local law prohibits in the way of landlord retaliation.** Don't assume that everything you do is protected.
- **Whenever possible, respond to retaliation by taking the offensive (filing in small claims court) rather than refusing to go along and risking an eviction.** That way, you avoid the notation on your credit record that you were involved in an eviction lawsuit, which will be damaging even if you win.
- **Enlist the support of fellow tenants.** Landlords will hesitate to strike back if they know that they're facing a solid group, not just one individual. Banding together is especially important if your state gives you little or no antiretaliation protection.

Chapter 12

Rent Control

Some cities and counties in California, Maryland, New Jersey, New York, and Washington, D.C. have laws that limit the amount of rent landlords may charge. Some of these ordinances also restrict the circumstances under which landlords may terminate month-to-month rental agreements or decide not to renew leases. Local rent control ordinances (also called "rent stabilization" or "maximum rent regulation" laws) are now in effect in some of the country's largest cities, including New York City, Washington, D.C., Los Angeles, San Francisco, Newark, San Jose, and Oakland.

Rent control ordinances vary widely. Some (like some of those in effect in New York) have real teeth, while others (in San Jose and Oakland, for example) are practically useless. And rent control is increasingly unpopular politically—so any changes to existing ordinances are likely to be pro-landlord. State law often restricts local rent control rules or bans them altogether; 32 states have laws prohibiting local rent control ordinances.

Because rent control ordinances are often extremely complex, we cannot give you a complete rundown of every feature. The summaries in Appendix 2 give you the basics, and "Where to Get Information About Rent Control," below, suggests further resources.

We can, however, explain common features found in most ordinances. Generally, these ordinances protect tenants by enhancing the pro-tenant provisions of already existing laws on landlord-tenant issues such as security deposits and evictions. Be sure to read the main chapter on each topic in conjunction with the rent control information here. For example, take a look at Chapter 4, "Security Deposits," along with Section D, below, explaining how rent control ordinances often add requirements and protections to a state's security deposit law.

TENANT TRAPS

Read this chapter to find out why you should:

- **Never assume that all rent control is alike.** Ordinances vary considerably, and the only way you can know whether you're protected in any particular situation is to read your local ordinance.
- **Never exercise any tenant right you may have under state law without checking to see whether your local rent control speaks to the issue, too.** While local ordinances can only add to—not decrease—your rights under state law, it's not wise to take action without knowing your local law on the issue. Many ordinances go beyond the regulation of rent and termination and have detailed provisions on other issues, such as security deposits.
- **Never agree with your landlord to circumvent the rent control law without giving it careful thought.** Once you've gone down that road, you may end up in worse shape.
- **Never bring in a roommate without your landlord's knowledge and consent.** This may give the landlord a prime opportunity to evict both of you when otherwise prohibited from doing so under the rent control law.

WHERE TO GET INFORMATION ABOUT RENT CONTROL

If you are protected by a rent control ordinance, get straight information from these resources:

- **Your city rent control board.** It can supply you with a copy of the current local ordinance, and possibly also with a brochure explaining the main features of the ordinance. The table "Selected Rent Control Ordinances" in Appendix 2 gives the addresses, phone numbers, and websites for the boards of seven major cities.
- **A local tenants' organization.** Virtually every city with a rent control ordinance has at least one active and vocal tenants' group. (In many cases, the pressure from these groups is why the city has rent control in the first place.) These organizations typically are vigorous watchdogs of the rent board and monitor court decisions and any political goings-on (such as proposed ballot amendments) that may affect the ordinance. Most important, tenant organizations can usually provide a written explanation of the ordinance and how it works, and many have volunteer staff available to explain ambiguous or complex facets of the ordinance. Some even provide free or low-cost legal services or assistance.
- **Local attorneys who specialize in landlord/tenant law.** If you have difficulty finding attorneys who will represent tenants (typically, there are more lawyers interested in representing landlords only), ask for referrals from a tenants' organization or any legal aid office.

A. Property Subject to Rent Control

Not all rental housing within a rent-controlled city is subject to rent control. Commonly, ordinances exempt:

- new buildings

- owner-occupied buildings with no more than three or four units
- single-family houses and luxury units that rent for more than a certain amount.

To find out whether your building is too new to fall within the statute, you'll need to look at the certificate of occupancy, issued after construction is complete and the inspectors have approved the work, on file in the local building inspector's office.

B. Limits on Rent

Rent control comes in two basic styles: one that protects only the present tenant, and one that regulates rent over the long term, regardless of turnover. In rent control jargon, these varieties are known respectively as "vacancy decontrol" (rent restrictions turn off when there's a new tenant) and "vacancy control" (rent restrictions remain in place when the unit rerents). The chart in Appendix 2 will tell you whether your ordinance provides for vacancy control or decontrol. Here's how they work.

1. Vacancy Decontrol Statutes: Protecting Current Tenants

Rent control may not be as great as you think—in most rent control areas, landlords may raise rent as much as they want when one tenant moves out and a new one moves in. This feature, called "vacancy decontrol" or "vacancy rent ceiling adjustment," means that rent control applies to a particular rental unit only as long as a particular tenant (or tenants) stays there. If a tenant voluntarily leaves or, in some cities, is evicted for a legal or "just" cause (discussed below), the rental unit is not subject to rent control again until the landlord sets the new (and presumably higher) rent. In short, in a "vacancy decontrol" city, don't expect to pay the same rent as the prior tenant.

In addition to built-in annual increases, most rent control boards allow landlords to petition for a rent hike based on an increase in costs, such as taxes or capital improvements like remodeling or bringing the building up to code.

2. Vacancy Control Statutes: Protecting Future Tenants

These rent control ordinances lock in the rent even when a unit turns over. The rent board sets a base rent for each rental unit, taking into account several factors, including the rent that was charged before rent control took effect, the landlord's operating and maintenance expenses, inflation, and housing supply and demand. The base rent may be raised during the tenancy under certain circumstances, such as an increase in inflation. When the tenant moves out, a landlord cannot raise the rent to market level. Rent stays controlled, subject to the formula of the rent control ordinance.

C. Evictions in Rent Control Areas

Tenancies normally end by their own accord: either at the end of a lease or after the proper amount of notice has been given in a month-to-month tenancy. As long as the landlord is not acting with discriminatory or retaliatory motives, the landlord can decide to call it quits, no reasons needed. (See Chapters 5 and 9.)

But for rent control to work—especially if the ordinance allows rents to rise when a tenant leaves—there must be added restrictions on eviction. Otherwise, landlords could throw out current tenants in order to get a chance to increase the rent. Recognizing this, many local ordinances require landlords to have a "just cause"—that is, a good reason—to evict. Acceptable reasons include:

- violating a significant term of the lease or rental agreement—for example, by failing to pay rent or allowing unauthorized people to live in the rental unit

- engaging in illegal activities on the premises, including drug dealing, substantial disturbance to the neighbors, or intentional damage to property
- a landlord's desire to move into the rental unit or give it to an immediate family member
- a landlord's desire to substantially remodel the property, which could not be done with people living there. Sometimes, a landlord must offer you another similar unit or give you first chance to move back in after the remodeling.

Landlords who violate these restrictions on evicting tenants often face stiff civil and even criminal penalties. Nonetheless, landlords in vacancy decontrol areas are fairly notorious for devising creative "just causes" to evict tenants—especially long-term ones—in order to get a chance to raise the rent to market rates. Sometimes it's easy for a landlord to find a reason to justify the eviction, such as pointing to an unauthorized pet. Other times, landlords try to turn a trivial offense into a just cause for the eviction, such as pointing to a single instance of rent arriving a day late as justifying a termination notice.

To prevent these types of disingenuous evictions, some rent control ordinances require that the stated reason for eviction be the landlord's "dominant motive." In other words, if you can prove that your one-day-late rent isn't the landlord's dominant motive, and that his desire to raise the rent is the true purpose behind the eviction, you may prevail in court. Of course, proving this—sometimes called a "bad faith eviction"—is often no easy task, and, even if you win, you'll undoubtedly have to devote precious time and money to defend yourself.

If you're facing a just cause eviction that you feel is a mere excuse for the landlord to raise the rent, one strategy is to fight aggressively to prevent the eviction lawsuit from being filed at all, starting with your first notice of the impending suit. Research your local ordinance and make it clear to your landlord in writing that you do not believe the eviction is legal, and that you plan to defend yourself to the full extent of the law. Emphasize whatever penalties exist in your area for violating the rent control law, and send copies of your correspondence to the rent board. In some areas such as San Francisco, you can file a complaint against your landlord with the rent board for wrongful eviction. While most rent control boards don't have the power to stop an eviction lawsuit filed in court, they may be able to dissuade a landlord from pursuing an eviction that has little merit by reminding the landlord of the law—and the potential penalties for violating it.

Rent control hearings can be time-consuming, expensive, and awful. Knowing how difficult a rent hearing can be, don't head for one if you have a weak case or none at all. Instead, consider trading your right to bring the landlord's eviction attempt before the rent board for a little extra time. For example, if you are being asked to move because of the impending arrival of the landlord's relative, you may well get an extension of a month or two in exchange for your promise not to challenge the legitimacy of the relative move-in. However, if you suspect an eviction is truly bogus, don't negotiate away your right to challenge it.

D. Interest Payments on Security Deposits

Local rent control ordinances sometimes impose rules regarding security deposits that supplement those set out by state law. For example, in Los Angeles and San Francisco, landlords are required to put security deposits in interest-bearing bank accounts, something not required under California *state* law. Check your ordinance to see whether similar protections apply to you. (Chapter 4 discusses interest payments on security deposits.)

E. Special Notice Requirements

State laws typically require landlords to give a specified amount of notice when it comes to raising the rent or terminating the tenancy. (Notice requirements in general are explained in Chapter 9.) In rent control situations, however, the notice requirements are often tighter in two situations:

- **Raising the rent.** State law often requires a 30-day notice for a rent increase. A local rent control law might also require the notice to inform the tenant that the rent control board can verify that the new rental amount is legal under the ordinance.
- **Terminating the tenancy.** Some rent control ordinances forbid the landlord from terminating (or refusing to renew) a tenancy without a "just cause," as explained above. And even where the landlord does have a just cause, the termination or nonrenewal period is often longer than that required under general state law.
- **Where to go for help.** Some rent control ordinances require the landlord to tell the tenant where to get information, such as from the local rent board or other administrative agency.

F. Bypassing the Rent Control Ordinance

Why does your landlord hate rent control? He doesn't like being told how to run his business, and he is sure that he would be making more money if he could set the rent at will. But he probably knows better than to defy the ordinance directly (maybe he's learned from sad experience). So how can he get around it?

One typical dodge is simply to reduce his operating expenses, thereby increasing his profit (if he turns off the sauna or forgoes a needed paint job, that's money saved). Many rent control ordinances address this ploy (under a doctrine known as "decrease in services") and allow you to challenge it directly by bringing it to the attention of the rent board. But there's another way a landlord can work this approach: Many landlords will barter needed maintenance for under-the-table rent. Or they will condition their approval of a perfectly reasonable request (such as giving approval for a new roommate or a sublet for the summer) on some added cash. Desperate for needed services or someone to share the rent, tenants often go along with the deal.

The consequences of playing outside the rules can be serious. For example, if you agree to pay under-the-table rent and are later evicted for failure to pay that rent, you *might* be able to survive the eviction by bringing to light the landlord's illegal circumvention of the rent control law. But you cannot know for sure whether a court will step in and save you from your foolishness and refuse to uphold your waiver. (If your midnight deal with the landlord is especially outrageous and offensive, your chances go up that a judge will throw it out.) In short, you may find yourself injured by your own bad deal.

So think carefully before agreeing to your landlord's scheme. Instead, bring the situation (lack of needed maintenance or a refusal to deal in good faith with your reasonable request for a roommate) to the attention of your rent board. If that proves futile and you agree to the deal, realize that there may be little you can do if the landlord reneges.

RULES TO RENT BY

- **Get a copy of your rent control ordinance and study it.** Rent control laws are often complex. Don't assume your landlord understands it.
- **Contact a local tenants' advocacy group.** Most rent-controlled cities have one or more tenant-oriented community organizations that are typically enthusiastic and savvy. You can get a lot of information on what goes on "under the hood" from them.
- **Watch out for landlord attempts to get around the ordinance.** Landlords frequently ask tenants to waive their rights under rent control, by asking for more money "under the table" in exchange for service or privileges. If you partake in one of these deals, understand that it's like making a pact with the devil—you may have nowhere to turn if the landlord doesn't come through.

Getting Help With Your Dispute

You're probably no stranger to a landlord-tenant dispute. Chances are, that's what brought you to this book in the first place. Hopefully, we've been able to give you the legal information you need to figure out whether you or the landlord has the stronger legal position. But knowing the law is one thing; knowing how to use it to your advantage is sometimes another.

It's rarely a good idea to go marching off to a lawyer's office or small claims court the minute you run up against an illegal policy or ploy of your landlord, no matter how legally correct your position may be. Negotiation, stressed repeatedly throughout this book, is cheaper, is usually less stressful, and often results in solutions that last. However, we are not so naïve as to think that every spat can be talked out over coffee and Danish. Sometimes you need help. Mediation and, if necessary, suing in small claims court are the next levels of engagement.

A. How to Negotiate a Settlement

No matter how serious the problem you face, you're almost always better off trying to resolve disputes directly with your landlord. You'll be most successful if you focus on exactly what you want the landlord to do, rather than fighting for the principle involved. Berating your landlord for insensitivity or ignorance may give you a sense of righteous vindication, but won't necessarily bring better results.

Here are some helpful pointers for negotiating with your landlord:

- Figure out ahead of time exactly you want to happen. Do you want to stay, or do you want out of your lease? Will you be satisfied with a sincere apology and pledge to do better, and can you trust the landlord to stick to his promises? Where are you willing to compromise? What's your bottom line?

- Set up an appointment to discuss the problem. Arrange a quiet time and place, preferably in a neutral location, where you can both express your concerns and work out an agreement.

- Let the landlord vent. Once the landlord starts talking, listen closely and don't interrupt, even if some points are not true or some opinions are inflammatory. Letting him get his version on the table tells him that you are willing to listen to his side—an essential first step towards an eventual understanding.

- State that you understand and respect the landlord's key points. Even if you strongly disagree with your landlord's position, it's often a good idea to restate his concerns as accurately as you can. This should discourage him from endlessly repeating the same point.

- Avoid personal attacks. Even if true, suggesting that your landlord is a slumlord or is profiteering at the expense of tenants will only raise the level of hostility and make settlement more difficult. Equally important, it's usually best to stay calm and not to react impulsively or emotionally to your landlord's misstatements.

- Be courteous, but not weak. If the law is on your side or you have the firm backing of most other tenants, let the landlord know that you're coming from a position of strength. Make it clear that you prefer negotiating an agreement but, if necessary, you have the resources and evidence to fight and win. If the issue concerns the landlord's failure to follow a state or local code, consider equipping yourself with a copy of the law, which you can show to him.

- Emphasize problem-solving. Try to structure the negotiation as a mutual attempt to solve a problem. For instance, if you're complaining about a landlord's policy of entering tenants' apartments to make unannounced repairs, seek solutions that recognize the interests of both parties—for example, an understanding that repairs are necessary and even desirable but that most can be prearranged.

- Put yourself in the landlord's loafers. How would you want to work with unhappy tenants if roles were reversed? Your answer may be something like, "I'd want to feel that I've won." As it turns out, this is a great insight—the best settlements are often those in which both sides feel they've won, or at least have not given up anything fundamental.

- If you reach an understanding with your landlord, promptly write it down and sign it. You should volunteer to prepare the first draft—not because you're a glutton for work, but because (as any savvy lawyer will tell you) she who drafts the document has the upper hand. If you agree to pay the landlord some money as part of the settlement, make it clear that the payment fully satisfies the landlord's claim: "Tenant's $200 payment of August 1, 200X, fully satisfies any claim Landlord has against Tenant regarding damaged patio furniture."

B. Using a Mediator

If you're unsuccessful negotiating a settlement with your landlord, or relations are so strained that no meeting seems possible, you may feel ready to give up on the idea of negotiation. This would be a mistake. Instead, the best approach is often to enlist the help of a neutral third-party mediator. Even if your landlord won't speak to you on the phone, a skilled and experienced mediator may get him to the table.

Many people confuse mediation with arbitration, a different legal tool that's seldom, if ever, used in residential landlord-tenant disputes. While both are nonjudicial ways to resolve disputes, there's a huge difference between them: Arbitration, like a lawsuit, results in a binding decision handed down by the arbitrator, who's like a judge. Mediators, by contrast, have no power to impose a decision. Their job is simply to help the parties work out a mutually acceptable solution to their dispute.

Put another way, if you and your landlord don't agree on a solution, there is no solution. However, if both sides desire to craft a resolution that *both* want to be binding, they can do so.

Mediation can make especially good sense if:

- Your landlord doesn't realize what a poor job the resident manager or management company has been doing, and you want the opportunity to bring this up.
- You are dealing with a good or at least halfway decent landlord, and you think there's hope for resolution.
- You think the landlord is savvy enough to want to avoid a protracted court battle.

Mediation can also help resolve roommate disputes. If you and your roommate disagree about noise, overnight guests, or some other issue, consider trying mediation.

Many skeptics are surprised to learn that mediation really does work. One big reason is the cooperative spirit that emerges. By agreeing to mediate a dispute in the first place, you and the landlord implicitly agree to solve your own problems. Also, the fact that no judge or arbitrator has the power to impose what may be an unacceptable solution reduces fear and defensiveness on both sides. This, in turn, often means both landlord and tenant take less extreme—and more conciliatory—positions.

The success of mediation in such a wide range of situations doesn't mean that it's always the right solution, however. Indeed, mediation is sometimes not the best approach. For example, if your landlord has discriminated against you based on your race, your sex, or some other illegal reason, you should probably file a fair housing complaint or a lawsuit, as explained in Chapter 5.

1. How to Find a Mediation Service

Many cities offer free or low-cost community mediation programs that handle landlord-tenant disputes. For information, call your mayor's or city manager's office and ask for the staff member who handles landlord-tenant mediation matters or housing disputes. That person should refer you to the public office or community group that attempts to resolve landlord-tenant disputes informally—and at little or no cost—before they reach the court stage. You can also get referrals for mediators from the American Arbitration Association (you'll see a list of regional offices by visiting their website at www.adr.org) or a neighborhood dispute resolution center. Colleges and universities often offer mediation services through their housing offices, especially when there is a large student population living in a relatively small town and the school has taken steps to address the quality of town-gown relations.

2. How Mediation Works

Mediation in landlord-tenant disputes is fairly informal. More likely than not, the mediator will have you and your landlord sit down together. Each side is usually asked to discuss all issues they consider important— even emotional ones. This process of airing the entire dispute often cools people off considerably and can lay the foundation for a fairly quick compromise.

If the dispute is not resolved easily, the mediator may suggest ways to resolve the problem, or may even keep everyone talking long enough to realize that the real problem goes deeper than the one being mediated. Typically this is helped along through a process called caucusing, in which each side occupies a separate, private room, with the mediator shuttling back and forth with offers and counteroffers. When settlement appears near, everyone gets back together and the mediator helps guide the parties to an agreement everyone approves.

For example, assume you and your landlord are in a tussle because you have threatened to withhold rent due to a serious defect in the premises, such as a broken heater. In a regular court hearing, this issue would be the only issue considered. In contrast, in the looser mediation process it may come to light that a major part of your grievance is that the manager has been slow to make all types of repairs, and the heat problem is simply the final straw.

You're not the only one who will have a chance to discuss peripheral issues. You may discover that your landlord is angry at you for letting your kids run wild and ruin the garden, or is sick and tired of getting calls from the police responding to noise complaints filed by your neighbors. Once all of this is on the table, a compromise solution may fall easily into place: You may agree to provide better supervision of your kids and cut out overly loud parties in exchange for the manager getting the heat fixed and doing other repairs quickly.

For more information on the mediation process, see *Mediate, Don't Litigate,* by Peter Lovenheim and Lisa Guerin (Nolo). This book explains mediation from start to finish, including how to get the other side to the mediation table (even if they oppose the idea), prepare for mediation, and draft a legally enforceable agreement.

C. Small Claims Court

If all else fails and you're ready to file a lawsuit, don't overlook the possibility of using small claims court. Unlike regular trial courts, these courts use simplified procedures that are much easier for people to handle without lawyers (in fact, in some states lawyers aren't even allowed to represent clients in small claims court).

Small claims court is most appropriate for disputes involving money, rather than disputes in which one side wants a judge to order the other to change his or her behavior. For example, arguments over security deposit refunds are prime candidates for small claims: There is a dispute as to whether the tenant damaged the property, left it a mess, or owes rent, and there is a sum of money at issue. The judge decides whom she believes and orders the money returned or not. If the money isn't returned as ordered, the victor can use that judgment (the official name for the judge's decision) to attach the loser's bank account or garnish his wages. The small claims judge won't be involved at that stage—she'll be busy hearing one of the dozens of other matters that pour into her courtroom each day.

A case whose resolution involves more than the payment of money, however, isn't always so neatly resolved. For instance, sexual harassment cases often result in orders that the harasser pay the victim damages *and* that the illegal behavior stop (often some counseling is required, too). If the harasser doesn't obey the judge's orders by reforming his behavior, the victim has to go back to court with her lawyers and ask the judge to enforce her decision (a judge might do this by slapping the loser with a contempt of court fine). Regular trial courts are often involved in enforcing their decisions, but small claims courts are not set up to do follow-up work. Consequently, small claims judges will hesitate to make orders that, if disobeyed, will land the parties back in their court again.

This said, there are still many landlord-tenant disputes that have monetary resolutions and are appropriate for small claims court. And often when a landlord learns (the hard way) that the consequences of his behavior are a stiff money judgment, he'll change that behavior. For instance, a landlord who fails to adequately maintain his property may get sued by a tenant who is injured by the defective conditions. After being ordered to pay the tenant for her medical bills and lost work, the landlord is likely to take care of business in the future.

If your case falls within the financial limits on small claims cases (in most states, you can't sue for more than a few thousand dollars), this route is a practical alternative to regular trial court. You can use small claims court to:

- force a landlord to follow through with promises in rental ads
- pressure a landlord to do minor repairs
- comply with an ordinance requiring the payment of interest on security deposits
- get your security deposit back.

1. Learning the Rules

Small claims court procedures are relatively simple and easy to master. Basically, you pay a small fee, file your lawsuit with the court clerk, see to it that the papers are served on your landlord (this can often be done by mail), show up on the appointed day, tell the judge your story, and present any witnesses and other evidence. Often the judge will announce her decision from the bench, or she may mail it to you within a short time.

Court rules that cover such things as where you file your lawsuit, how legal papers must be delivered to your opponent ("service of process"), and how promptly you must sue are usually available from the small claims clerk. In addition, clerks in small claims court are expected to explain procedures to you. In some states, they may even help you fill out the necessary forms, which are quite simple anyhow. If necessary, be persistent in your requests for assistance. If you ask enough questions, you'll get the answers you need to handle your own case comfortably. Also, in some states such as California, you can consult a free small claims court adviser.

2. Financial Caps on Small Claims Cases

Exactly how much can you sue for in small claims court? The maximum varies from state to state. In most, it is $3,000 to $4,000. Call your local court clerk and ask for the small claims division, which will be able to give you this information.

Keep in mind that it may make sense to scale back your claim to fit within the small claims limit, rather than suing for the entire amount in regular trial court. By the time you pay your lawyer and court costs, you may find that you would have come out ahead had you chosen small claims in the first place.

3. How to Win

Showing up with persuasive evidence that supports your story is the way to win in small claims court. For example, if you are suing your landlord to get your security deposit returned, you'll want to have a photograph of a clean and undamaged apartment and the convincing testimony of someone who helped you clean up.

Luckily, you don't have to be a Harvard-trained lawyer to present your evidence, either. People in small claims court aren't usually held to the picky and difficult-to-understand rules of formal court. For example, a judge may be willing to listen to your account of what a repairman had to say about the condition of the furnace in your frigid flat—in formal court, you'd hardly get the words out before the other side would yell "Hearsay!" and shut you down. That's not to say, however, that the judge will necessarily *believe* that the repairperson in fact said what you claim he did. It's far better to have a written, signed statement from the repairperson, which dispels any suggestion that you are making it all up.

Everybody's Guide to Small Claims Court, by Ralph Warner (Nolo), provides detailed advice on bringing or defending a small claims court case, preparing evidence and witnesses for court, and collecting your money judgment when you win. Especially if you have never been to small claims court, you'll want to closely study the material on how to present your testimony and witnesses in court. *Everybody's Guide to Small Claims Court* will also be useful in defending yourself against a landlord who sues you in small claims court—for example, claiming that you owe money for damage to the premises.

RULES TO RENT BY

If you and your landlord are at odds, plan your approach carefully. Keep in mind:

- **You'll catch more flies with honey than with vinegar.** Unless you're facing someone with a Neanderthal's sensitivity, start with a willingness to listen to the landlord's position, however much you disagree. Then explain your side and the (hopefully) persuasive legal reasons you have to back you up.
- **Try mediation before hustling off to court.** Even if the landlord refuses, it's to your advantage to be able to say later to a judge, "I tried to get the landlord to participate but he wouldn't budge."
- **Document every move in a landlord-tenant dispute as if it is, in fact, heading for court.** For example, save copies of letters (and send them certified), take photos, and memorialize conversations in letters of understanding. (See Chapter 2, Section G.) If you don't need to go to court, fine; but if all else fails, you will appreciate knowing that you've amassed helpful evidence.
- **If you and the landlord reach a decision, write it down and ask the landlord to review your draft and sign it.**

Appendix I

How to Find
Landlord-Tenant Laws Online

Every tenant is covered by state, local, and federal law. In some areas, like antidiscrimination standards, laws overlap. When they do, the stricter laws will apply. In practical terms, this usually means that the laws that give tenants the most protection (rights and remedies) will prevail over less-protective laws.

You can get the text of every federal and state statute (except Louisiana) free, online. Rules put out by federal and state regulatory agencies are often available, too, and the Internet's legal resources grow every day. We list the websites where you can get your hands on legal information below.

A. State Laws

As a tenant, you'll be primarily concerned with state law. State statutes cover many aspects of the landlord-tenant relationship, including deposits, privacy, discrimination, housing standards, rent rules, repair and maintenance rights and responsibilities, and eviction procedures. We include citations for the major state landlord-tenant laws in Appendix 2 so that you can do additional research.

You can easily find state statutes online by going to Nolo's home page at www.nolo.com. Click under "Legal Research Center," where it says "49 State Laws." Then click on the name of your state to find a particular statute.

If you know the statute's number or citation (available in the charts in Appendix 2 of this book), you can go directly there. If you don't know the statute number, you can enter a "keyword" that is likely to be in it, such as "deposit" or "security deposit." If you just want to browse through the statutes, you can search the table of contents for your state's laws. With a little trial and error, you should have no trouble finding a particular landlord-tenant statute.

Don't forget to check your state consumer protection agency or attorney general's office—many provide useful publications explaining state laws that affect tenants.

B. Local Ordinances

Local ordinances, such as rent control rules and health and safety standards, also affect tenants.

Many municipalities have local ordinances online. Go to www.statelocalgov.net and search for the name of a particular city. Sometimes this presence is nothing more than a not-so-slick public relations page, but often it includes a large body of information, including local ordinances available for searching and downloading.

Finally, your local public library or office of the city attorney, mayor, or city manager can provide information on local ordinances that affect tenants.

If your rental unit is rent-regulated, be sure to get a copy of the ordinance, as well as all rules issued by the rent board covering rent increases and hearings.

C. Federal Statutes and Regulations

Congress has enacted laws, and federal agencies such as the U.S. Department of Housing and Urban Development (HUD) have adopted regulations, covering discrimination and other issues affecting tenants, such as disclosure of environmental health hazards. We include citations for some of the key federal laws affecting tenants throughout this book. The U.S. Code is the starting place for most federal statutory research. To access the U.S. Code online, see the Cornell Law Information Institute at www.law.cornell.edu.

THE BASICS OF LEGAL RESEARCH

Nolo's Legal Research Center at www.nolo.com provides an overview of legal research. If you want to go further, we recommend *Legal Research: How to Find and Understand the Law,* by Stephen Elias and Susan Levinkind (Nolo). This nontechnical book gives easy-to-use step-by-step instructions on how to find legal information.

Appendix 2

State Laws and Agencies

State Landlord-Tenant Statutes

Here are some of the key statutes pertaining to landlord-tenant law in each state. In some states, important legal principles are contained in court opinions, not codes or statutes. Court-made law is not reflected in this chart.

State	Statute	State	Statute
Alabama	Ala. Code §§ 35-9-1 to 35-9-100	Montana	Mont. Code Ann. §§ 70-24-101 to 70-25-206
Alaska	Alaska Stat. §§ 34.03.010 to 34.03.380	Nebraska	Neb. Rev. Stat. §§ 76-1401 to 76-1449
Arizona	Ariz. Rev. Stat. Ann. §§ 12-1171 to 12-1183, § 33-1301 to 33-1381	Nevada	Nev. Rev. Stat. Ann. §§ 118A.010 to 118A.520
Arkansas	Ark. Code Ann. §§ 18-16-101 to 18-16-306	New Hampshire	N.H. Rev. Stat. Ann. §§ 540:1 to 540:29, 540-A:1 to 540-A:8
California	Cal. Civ. Code §§ 1925 to 1954, 1961 to 1962.7	New Jersey	N.J. Stat. Ann. §§ 46:8-1 to 46:8-49
Colorado	Colo. Rev. Stat. §§ 38-12-101 to 38-12-104, 38-12-301 to 38-12-302	New Mexico	N.M. Stat. Ann. §§ 47-8-1 to 47-8-51
Connecticut	Conn. Gen. Stat. Ann. §§ 47a-1 to 47a-51	New York*	N.Y. Real Prop. Law §§ 220 to 238; Real Prop. Acts. §§ 701 to 853; Mult. Dwell. Law (all); Mult. Res. Law (all); Gen. Oblig. Law §§ 7-103 to 7-108
Delaware	Del. Code Ann. tit. 25, §§ 5101 to 7013	North Carolina	N.C. Gen. Stat. §§ 42-1 to 42-14.2, 42-25.6 to 42-76
Dist. of Columbia	D.C. Code Ann. §§ 42-3201 to 42-3610; D.C. Mun. Regs., tit. 14, §§ 300 to 311	North Dakota	N.D. Cent. Code §§ 47-16-01 to 47-16-41
Florida	Fla. Stat. Ann. §§ 83.40 to 83.682	Ohio	Ohio Rev. Code Ann. §§ 5321.01 to 5321.19
Georgia	Ga. Code Ann. §§ 44-7-1 to 44-7-81	Oklahoma	Okla. Stat. Ann. tit. 41, §§ 101 to 136
Hawaii	Haw. Rev. Stat. §§ 521-1 to 521-78	Oregon	Or. Rev. Stat. §§ 90.100 to 90.450
Idaho	Idaho Code §§ 6-301 to 6-324, 55-208 to 55-308	Pennsylvania	68 Pa. Cons. Stat. Ann. §§ 250.101 to 250.510-B
Illinois	765 Ill. Comp. Stat. §§ 705/0.01 to 740/5	Rhode Island	R.I. Gen. Laws §§ 34-18-1 to 34-18-57
Indiana	Ind. Code Ann. §§ 32-31-1-1 to 32-31-8-6	South Carolina	S.C. Code Ann. §§ 27-40-10 to 27-40-910
Iowa	Iowa Code Ann. §§ 562A.1 to 562A.36	South Dakota	S.D. Codified Laws Ann. §§ 43-32-1 to 43-32-29
Kansas	Kan. Stat. Ann. §§ 58-2501 to 58-2573	Tennessee	Tenn. Code Ann. §§ 66-28-101 to 66-28-521
Kentucky	Ky. Rev. Stat. Ann. §§ 383.010 to 383.715	Texas	Tex. Prop. Code Ann. §§ 91.001 to 92.354
Louisiana	La. Rev. Stat. Ann. §§ 9:3251 to 9:3259; La. Civ. Code Ann. art. 2668 to 2742	Utah	Utah Code Ann. §§ 57-17-1 to 57-17-5, 57-22-1 to 57-22-6
Maine	Me. Rev. Stat. Ann. tit. 14, §§ 6001 to 6046	Vermont	Vt. Stat. Ann. tit. 9, §§ 4451 to 4468
Maryland	Md. Code Ann. [Real Prop.] §§ 8-101 to 8-604	Virginia	Va. Code Ann. §§ 55-218.1 to 55-248.40
Massachusetts	Mass. Gen. Laws Ann. ch. 186, §§ 1 to 21	Washington	Wash. Rev. Code Ann. §§ 59.04.010 to 59.04.900, 59.18.010 to 59.18.911
Michigan	Mich. Comp. Laws §§ 554.601 to 554.641	West Virginia	W. Va. Code §§ 37-6-1 to 37-6-30
Minnesota	Minn. Stat. Ann. §§ 504B.001 to 504B.471	Wisconsin	Wis. Stat. Ann. §§ 704.01 to 704.50
Mississippi	Miss. Code Ann. §§ 89-8-1 to 89-8-27	Wyoming	Wyo. Stat. §§ 1-21-1201 to 1-21-1211, 34-2-128 to 34-2-129
Missouri	Mo. Rev. Stat. §§ 441.005 to 441.880, 535.150 to 535.300		

* See *The New York Landlord's Law Book*, by Mary Ann Hallenborg (Nolo), for details on rent stabilization—and rent control—laws and regulations in New York State and New York City.

State Rent Rules

Here are citations for statues that set out rent rules in each state. When a state has no statute, the space is left blank. See the "Notice Required to Change or Terminate a Month-to-Month Tenancy" chart in this appendix for citations to raising rent.

State	When Rent Is Due	Grace Period	Where Rent Is Due	Late Fees
Alabama				
Alaska	Alaska Stat. § 34.03.020(c)		Alaska Stat. § 34.03.020(c)	
Arizona	Ariz. Rev. Stat. Ann. § 33-1314(C)	Ariz. Rev. Stat. Ann. § 33-1368(B)	Ariz. Rev. Stat. Ann. § 33-1314(C)	Ariz. Rev. Stat. Ann. § 33-1368(B)
Arkansas				
California	Cal. Civil Code § 1947		Cal. Civil Code § 1962	*Orozco v. Casimiro*, 212 Cal. App. 4th Supp. 7 (2004)
Colorado				
Connecticut	Conn. Gen. Stat. Ann. § 47a-3a	Conn. Gen. Stat. Ann. § 47a-15a	Conn. Gen. Stat. Ann. § 47a-3a	Conn. Gen. Stat. Ann. § 47a-4(a)(8)
Delaware	Del. Code Ann. tit. 25, § 5501(b)	Del. Code Ann. tit. 25, § 5501(d)	Del. Code Ann. tit. 25, § 5501(b)	Del. Code Ann. tit. 25, § 5501(d)
D.C.				
Florida	Fla. Stat. Ann. § 83.46(1)			
Georgia				
Hawaii	Haw. Rev. Stat. § 521-21(b)		Haw. Rev. Stat. § 521-21(b)	
Idaho				
Illinois				
Indiana	*Watson v. Penn*, 108 Ind. 21, 8 N.E. 636 (1886)			
Iowa	Iowa Code Ann. § 562A.9(3)		Iowa Code Ann. § 562A.9(3)	Iowa Code Ann. § 535.2(7)
Kansas	Kan. Stat. Ann. § 58-2545(c)		Kan. Stat. Ann. § 58-2545(c)	
Kentucky	Ky. Rev. Stat. Ann. § 383.565(2)		Ky. Rev. Stat. Ann. § 383.565(2)	
Louisiana*	La. Civ. Code art. 2703(1)		La. Civ. Code art. 2703(2)	
Maine		Me. Rev. Stat. Ann. tit. 14, § 6028		Me. Rev. Stat. Ann. tit. 14, § 6028
Maryland				Md. Code Ann. [Real Prop.] § 8-208(d)(3)
Massachusetts		Mass. Gen. Laws Ann. ch. 186 § 15B(1)(c)		Mass. Gen. Laws Ann. ch. 186 § 15B(1)(c)
Michigan	*Hilsendegen v. Scheich*, 21 N.W. 894 (1885)			

* Effective 1/1/2005.

State Rent Rules (continued)

State	When Rent Is Due	Grace Period	Where Rent Is Due	Late Fees
Minnesota				
Mississippi				
Missouri	Mo. Rev. Stat. § 535.060			
Montana	Mont. Code Ann. § 70-24-201(2)(c)		Mont. Code Ann. § 70-24-201(2)(b)	
Nebraska	Neb. Rev. Stat. § 76-1414(3)		Neb. Rev. Stat. § 76-1414(3)	
Nevada	Nev. Rev. Stat. Ann. §§ 118A.210			Nev. Rev. Stat. Ann. § 118A.200(2)(g), (3)(c)
New Hampshire				
New Jersey				N.J. Stat. Ann. § 2A:42-6.1
New Mexico	N.M. Stat. Ann. § 47-8-15(B)		N.M. Stat. Ann. § 47-8-15(B)	N.M. Stat. Ann § 47-8-15(D)
New York*				
North Carolina		N.C. Gen Stat. § 42-46		N.C. Gen. Stat. § 42-46
North Dakota	N.D. Cent. Code § 47-16-20			
Ohio				
Oklahoma	Okla. Stat. Ann. tit. 41, § 109		Okla. Stat. Ann. tit. 41, § 109	*Sun Ridge Investors Ltd. v. Parker*, 956 P.2d 876 (1998)
Oregon	Or. Rev. Stat. § 90.240(6)(a)	Or. Rev. Stat. § 90.260	Or. Rev. Stat. § 90.240(6)(a)	Or. Rev. Stat. § 90.260
Pennsylvania				
Rhode Island	R.I. Gen. Laws § 34-18-15(c)	R.I. Gen. Laws § 34-18-35	R.I. Gen. Laws § 34-18-15(c)	
South Carolina	S.C. Code Ann. § 27-40-310(c)		S.C. Code Ann. § 27-40-310(c)	
South Dakota	S.D. Codified Laws Ann. § 43-32-12			
Tennessee	Tenn. Code Ann. § 66-28-201(c)	Tenn. Code Ann. § 66-28-201(d)	Tenn. Code Ann. § 66-28-201(c)	Tenn. Code Ann. § 66-28-201(d)
Texas				
Utah				
Vermont	Vt. Stat. Ann. tit. 9, § 4455			
Virginia	Va. Code Ann. § 55-248.7(C)			
Washington	Wash. Rev. Code Ann. § 59.18.130			
West Virginia				
Wisconsin				
Wyoming				

* See *The New York Landlord's Law Book*, by Mary Ann Hallenborg (Nolo), for details on rent stabilization and rent control laws and regulations in New York State and New York City.

Notice Required to Change or Terminate a Month-to-Month Tenancy

Except where noted, the amount of notice a landlord must give to increase rent or change another term of the rental agreement in month-to-month tenancy is the same as that required to end a month-to-month tenancy. Be sure to check state and local rent control laws, which may have different notice requirements.

State	Tenant	Landlord	Statute	Comments
Alabama	10 days	10 days	Ala. Code § 35-9-3	No state statute on the amount of notice required to change rent or other terms.
Alaska	30 days	30 days	Alaska Stat. § 34.03.290(b)	
Arizona	30 days	30 days	Ariz. Rev. Stat. Ann. § 33-1375	
Arkansas	10 days	10 days	Ark. Code Ann. § 18-16-101	
California	30 days	30 or 60 days	Cal. Civ. Code § 1946; Cal. Civ. Code § 827a	30 days to change rental terms, but if landlord is raising the rent, tenant gets 60 days' notice if the sum of this and all prior rent increases during the previous 12 months is more than 10% of the lowest rent charged during that time. 60 days to terminate (landlord), 30 days (tenant).
Colorado			No statute	
Connecticut			No statute	
Delaware	60 days	60 days	Del. Code Ann. tit. 25, §§ 5106, 5107	After receiving notice of landlord's proposed change terms, tenant has 15 days to terminate tenancy. Otherwise, changes will take effect as announced.
District of Columbia	30 days	30 days	D.C. Code Ann. § 42-3202	No state statute on the amount of notice required to change rent or other terms.
Florida	15 days	15 days	Fla. Stat. Ann. § 83.57	No state statute on the amount of notice required to change rent or other terms.
Georgia	30 days	60 days	Ga. Code Ann. § 44-7-7	No state statute on the amount of notice required to change rent or other terms.
Hawaii	28 days	45 days	Haw. Rev. Stat. §§ 521-71, 521-21(d)	
Idaho	One month	One month	Idaho Code §§ 55-208, 55-307	Landlords must provide 15 days' notice to increase rent or change tenancy.
Illinois	30 days	30 days	735 Ill. Comp. Stat. § 5/9-207	
Indiana	One month	One month	Ind. Code Ann. § 32-31-1-1	
Iowa	30 days	30 days	Iowa Code Ann. §§ 562A.34, 562A.13(5)	
Kansas	30 days	30 days	Kan. Stat. Ann. § 58-2570	No state statute on the amount of notice required to change rent or other terms.
Kentucky	30 days	30 days	Ky. Rev. Stat. Ann. § 383.695	
Louisiana	10 days	10 days	La. Civ. Code Art. 2720	No state statute on the amount of notice required to change rent or other terms.
Maine	30 days	30 days	Me. Rev. Stat. Ann. tit. 14 §§ 6002, 6015	Landlord must provide 45 days' notice to increase rent.
Maryland	One month	One month	Md. Code Ann. [Real Prop.] § 8-402(b)(3), (b)(4)	Two months, notice required in Montgomery County. Does not apply in Baltimore.
Massachusetts	See 1 below	See 1 below	Mass. Gen. Laws Ann. ch. 186, § 12	
Michigan	See 2 below	See 2 below	Mich. Comp. Laws § 554.134	No state statute on the amount of notice required to change rent or other terms.
Minnesota	See 3 below	See 3 below	Minn. Stat. Ann. § 504B.135	No state statute on the amount of notice required to change rent or other terms.
Mississippi	30 days	30 days	Miss. Code Ann. § 89-8-19	No state statute on the amount of notice required to change rent or other terms.
Missouri	One month	One month	Mo. Rev. Stat. § 441.060	No state statute on the amount of notice required to change rent or other terms.
Montana	30 days	30 days	Mont. Code Ann. § 70-24-441	No state statute on the amount of notice required to change rent or other terms.

1. Interval between days of payment or 30 days, whichever is longer.
2. Interval between times of payment.
3. Interval between time rent is due.

Notice Required to Change or Terminate a Month-to-Month Tenancy (continued)

State	Tenant	Landlord	Statute	Comments
Nebraska	30 days	30 days	Neb. Rev. Stat. § 76-1437	No state statute on the amount of notice required to change rent or other terms.
Nevada	30 days	30 days	Nev. Rev. Stat. Ann. §§ 40.251, 118A.300	Landlords must provide 45 days' notice to increase rent.
New Hampshire	30 days	30 days	N.H. Rev. Stat. Ann. §§ 540:2, 540:3	Landlord may terminate only for just cause.
New Jersey			No statute	
New Mexico	30 days	30 days	N.M. Stat. Ann. §§ 47-8-37, 47-8-15(F)	Landlord must deliver rent increase notice at least 30 days before rent due date.
New York*	One month	One month	N.Y. Real Prop. Law § 232-b	No state statute on the amount of notice required to change rent or other terms.
North Carolina	7 days	7 days	N.C. Gen. Stat. § 42-14	No state statute on the amount of notice required to change rent or other terms.
North Dakota	30 days	30 days	N.D. Cent. Code § 47-16-15	Tenant may terminate with 25 days' notice if landlord has changed the terms of the lease.
Ohio	30 days	30 days	Ohio Rev. Code Ann. § 5321.17	No state statute on the amount of notice required to change rent or other terms.
Oklahoma	30 days	30 days	Okla. Stat. Ann. tit. 41, § 111	No state statute on the amount of notice required to change rent or other terms.
Oregon	30 days	30 days	Or. Rev. Stat. § 91.070	No state statute on the amount of notice required to change rent or other terms.
Pennsylvania			No statute	
Rhode Island	30 days	30 days	R.I. Gen. Laws §§ 34-18-16.1, 34-18-37	Landlord must provide 30 days' notice to increase rent.
South Carolina	30 days	30 days	S.C. Code Ann. § 27-40-770	No state statute on the amount of notice required to change rent or other terms.
South Dakota	One month	One month	S.D. Codified Laws Ann. §§ 43-32-13, 43-8-8	Tenant may terminate within 15 days of receiving landlord's modification notice.
Tennessee	30 days	30 days	Tenn. Code Ann. § 66-28-512	No state statute on the amount of notice required to change rent or other terms.
Texas	One month	One month	Tex. Prop. Code Ann. § 91.001	No state statute on the amount of notice required to change rent or other terms.
Utah			No statute	
Vermont	One rental period	30 days	Vt. Code Ann. tit. 9, §§ 4467, 4456(d)	If there is no written rental agreement, for tenants who have continuously resided in the unit for two years or less, 60 days' notice to terminate; for those who have resided longer than two years, 90 days. If there is a written rental agreement, for tenants who have lived continuously in the unit for two years or less, 30 days; for those who have lived there longer than two years, 60 days.
Virginia	30 days	30 days	Va. Code Ann. §§ 55-248.37, 55-248.7	No state statute on the amount of notice required to change rent or other terms, but landlord must abide by notice provisions in the rental agreement, if any, and tenant must consent in writing to any change.
Washington	30 days	20 days	Wash. Rev. Code Ann. §§ 59.18.200, 59.18.140	Landlord must give 30 days to change rent or other lease terms.
West Virginia	One month	One month	W. Va. Code § 37-6-5	No state statute on the amount of notice required to change rent or other terms.
Wisconsin	28 days	28 days	Wis. Stat. Ann. § 704.19	No state statute on the amount of notice required to change rent or other terms.
Wyoming			No statute	

* See *The New York Landlord's Law Book*, by Mary Ann Hallenborg (Nolo), for details on rent stabilization—and rent control —laws and regulations in New York State and New York City.

State Security Deposit Rules

Here are citations for statutes pertaining to security deposits in each state. Details on various aspects of security deposits are provided in the chapters.

This table is limited to security deposit statutes. Some states—Alabama and West Virginia—do not have statutes on security deposits. That doesn't mean that there is no law on the subject. Court decisions (what lawyers call "case law")

in your state may set out quite specific requirements for refunding of deposits, whether they should be held in interest-bearing accounts, and the like. This book does not cover all case or local law. To find out whether courts or local governments in your state have made decisions or ordinances you need to be aware of, you may need to do some legal research on your own.

State	Statute	Limit	Separate Account	Interest	Deadline for Landlord to Itemize and Return Deposit	Exemptions
Alabama	No statute					
Alaska	Alaska Stat. § 34.03.070	Two months' rent, where rent exceeds $2,000 per month	✔		14 days if the tenant gives proper notice to terminate tenancy; 30 days if the tenant does not give proper notice	Any rental unit where the rent exceeds $2,000 per month
Arizona	Ariz. Rev. Stat. Ann. § 33-1321	One and one-half months' rent (unless tenant voluntarily agrees to pay more)			14 days	
Arkansas	Ark. Code Ann. §§ 18-16-303 to 18-16-306	Two months' rent			30 days	Landlord who owns five or fewer rental units, unless these units are managed by a third party for a fee
California	Cal. Civ. Code §§ 1950.5, 1940.5(g)	Two months' rent (unfurnished); three months' rent (furnished). Add extra one-half month's rent for waterbed			Three weeks	
Colorado	Colo. Rev. Stat. §§ 38-12-102 to 38-12-104	No statutory limit			One month, unless lease agreement specifies longer period of time (which may be no more than 60 days); 72 hours (not counting weekends or holidays) if a hazardous condition involving gas equipment requires tenant to vacate	
Connecticut	Conn. Gen. Stat. Ann. § 47a-21	Two months' rent (tenant under 62 years of age); one month's rent (tenant 62 years of age or older)	✔	✔	30 days, or within 15 days of receiving tenant's forwarding address, whichever is later	
Delaware	Del. Code. Ann. tit. 25, § 5514	One month's rent on leases for one year or more; no limit for month-to-month rental agreements (may require additional pet deposit of up to one month's rent)	✔		20 days	

State Security Deposit Rules (continued)

State	Statute	Limit	Separate Account	Interest	Deadline for Landlord to Itemize and Return Deposit	Exemptions
District of Columbia	D.C. Code Ann. § 42-3502.17; D.C. Mun. Regs. tit. 14, §§ 308 to 311	One month's rent	✔	✔	45 days	
Florida	Fla. Stat. Ann. §§ 83.49, 83.43 (12)	No statutory limit	✔	[1]	15 to 60 days depending on whether tenant disputes deductions	
Georgia	Ga. Code Ann. §§ 44-7-30 to 44-7-37	No statutory limit	✔		One month	Landlord who owns ten or fewer rental units, unless these units are managed by an outside party
Hawaii	Haw. Rev. Stat. §§ 521-44, 521-42	One month's rent			14 days	
Idaho	Idaho Code § 6-321	No statutory limit			21 days or up to 30 days if landlord and tenant agree	
Illinois	765 Ill. Comp. Stat. 710/0.01 to 715/3	No statutory limit		✔ [2]	30 to 45 days depending on whether tenant disputes deductions	Landlord who owns four or fewer dwelling units
Indiana	Ind. Code Ann. §§ 32-31-3-9 to 32-31-3-19	No statutory limit			45 days	
Iowa	Iowa Code Ann. § 562A.12	Two months' rent	✔	[1]	30 days	
Kansas	Kan. Stat. Ann. §§ 58-2550, 58-2548	One month's rent (unfurnished); one and one-half months' rent (furnished); for pets, add extra one-half month's rent			30 days	
Kentucky	Ky. Rev. Stat. Ann. § 383.580	No statutory limit	✔		30 to 60 days depending on whether tenant disputes deductions	
Louisiana	La. Rev. Stat. Ann. §§ 9:3251 to 9:3254	No statutory limit			One month	
Maine	Me. Rev. Stat. Ann. tit. 14, §§ 6031 to 6038	Two months' rent	✔		30 days (if written rental agreement) or 21 days (if tenancy at will)	Rental unit which is part of structure with five or fewer units, one of which is occupied by landlord
Maryland	Md. Code Ann. [Real Prop.] § 8-203, 8-203.1	Two months' rent	✔	✔	30 to 45 days depending on whether tenant has been evicted or has abandoned the premises	
Massachusetts	Mass. Gen. Laws Ann. ch. 186, § 15B	One month's rent	✔	✔	30 days	
Michigan	Mich. Comp. Laws §§ 554.602 to 554.613	One and one-half months' rent	✔		30 days	

[1] Interest payments are not required, but when they are made, certain rules apply.
[2] Applies only to landlords with 25 or more rental units.

State Security Deposit Rules (continued)

State	Statute	Limit	Separate Account	Interest	Deadline for Landlord to Itemize and Return Deposit	Exemptions
Minnesota	Minn. Stat. Ann. §§ 504B.175 to 504B.178	No statutory limit		✔	Three weeks after tenant leaves and landlord receives forwarding address; five days if tenant must leave due to building condemnation	
Mississippi	Miss. Code Ann. § 89-8-21	No statutory limit			45 days	
Missouri	Mo. Ann. Stat. § 535.300	Two months' rent			30 days	
Montana	Mont. Code Ann. §§ 70-25-101 to 70-25-206	No statutory limit			30 days; 10 days if no deductions	
Nebraska	Neb. Rev. Stat. § 76-1416	One month's rent (no pets); one and one-quarter months' rent (pets)			14 days	
Nevada	Nev. Rev. Stat. Ann. §§ 118A.240 to 118A.250	Three months' rent			30 days	
New Hampshire	N.H. Rev. Stat. Ann §§ 540-A:5 to 540-A:8; 540-B:10	One month's rent or $100, whichever is greater; when landlord and tenant share facilities, no statutory limit	✔	✔	30 days For shared facilities, if the deposit is more than 30 days' rent, landlord must provide written agreement acknowledging receipt and specifying when deposit will be returned. If no written agreement, 20 days after tenant vacates	Landlord who leases a single-family residence and owns no other rental property, or landlord who leases rental units in an owner-occupied building of five units or less (exemption does not apply to any individual unit in owner-occupied building that is occupied by a person 60 years of age or older)
New Jersey	N.J. Stat. Ann. §§ 46:8-19 to 46:8-26	One and one-half months' rent	✔	✔	30 days; five days in case of fire, flood, condemnation, or evacuation	Owner-occupied building with two or fewer units where tenant fails to provide 30 days' written notice to landlord invoking provisions of act
New Mexico	N.M. Stat. Ann. §§ 47-8-18	One month's rent (for rental agreement of less than one year); no limit for leases of one year or more		✔	30 days	
New York [3]	N.Y. Gen. Oblig. Law §§ 7-103 to 7-108	No statutory limit for nonregulated units	✔	✔	Reasonable time	Landlord who rents out nonregulated units in buildings with five or fewer units need not pay interest
North Carolina	N.C. Gen. Stat. §§ 42-50 to 42-56	One and one-half months' rent for month-to-month rental agreements; two months' rent if term is longer than two months	✔		30 days	

[3] See *The New York Landlord's Law Book*, by Mary Ann Hallenborg (Nolo), for details on rent stabilization—and rent control—laws and regulations in New York State and New York City.

State Security Deposit Rules (continued)

State	Statute	Limit	Separate Account	Interest	Deadline for Landlord to Itemize and Return Deposit	Exemptions
North Dakota	N.D. Cent. Code §§ 47-16-07.1, 47-16-07.2	One month's rent (or $1,500 if tenant has a pet)	✔	✔	30 days	
Ohio	Ohio Rev. Code Ann. § 5321.16	No statutory limit		✔	30 days	
Oklahoma	Okla. Stat. Ann. tit. 41, § 115	No statutory limit	✔		30 days	
Oregon	Or. Rev. Stat. § 90.300	No statutory limit			31 days	
Pennsylvania	68 Pa. Cons. Stat. Ann. §§ 250.511a to 250.512	Two months' rent for first year of renting; one month's rent during second and subsequent years of renting	✔	✔	30 days	
Rhode Island	R.I. Gen. Laws § 34-18-19	One month's rent			20 days	
South Carolina	S.C. Code Ann. § 27-40-410	No statutory limit			30 days	
South Dakota	S.D. Codified Laws Ann. § 43.32-6.1, § 43-32-24	One month's rent (higher deposit may be charged if special conditions pose a danger to maintenance of the premises)			Two weeks to return entire deposit or a portion, and supply reasons for withholding; 45 days for a written, itemized accounting, if tenant requests it	
Tennessee	Tenn. Code Ann. § 66-28-301	No statutory limit	✔		No statutory deadline to return; 10 days to itemize	
Texas	Tex. Prop. Code Ann. §§ 92.101 to 92.109	No statutory limit			30 days	
Utah	Utah Code Ann. §§ 57-17-1 to 57-17-5	No statutory limit			30 days, or within 15 days of receiving tenant's forwarding address, whichever is later	
Vermont	Vt. Stat. Ann. tit. 9, § 4461	No statutory limit			14 days	
Virginia	Va. Code Ann. §§ 55-248.11:1, 55-248.15:1	Two months' rent		✔	45 days	
Washington	Wash. Rev. Code Ann. §§ 59.18.260 to 59.18.285	No statutory limit	✔		14 days	
W. Virginia	No statute					
Wisconsin	Wis. Admin. Code ATCP 134.06	No statutory limit			21 days	
Wyoming	Wyo. Stat. §§ 1-21-1207 to 1-21-1208	No statutory limit			30 days, or within 15 days of receiving tenant's forwarding address, whichever is later; 60 days if there is damage	

State Laws on Rent Withholding and Repair and Deduct Remedies

Here are citations for state laws that allow tenants to withhold rent or use the repair and deduct remedy for landlord's failure to provide habitable premises or supply essential services.

State	Statute or Case on Rent Withholding	Statute or Case on Repair and Deduct
Alabama	No statute	No statute
Alaska	Alaska Stat. § 34.03.190	Alaska Stat. § 34.03.180
Arizona	Ariz. Rev. Stat. Ann. § 33-1365	Ariz. Rev. Stat. Ann. §§ 33-1363 to -1364
Arkansas	No statute	No statute
California	*Green v. Superior Court*, 10 Cal. 3d 616 (1974)	Cal. Civ. Code § 1942
Colorado	No statute	No statute
Connecticut	Conn. Gen. Stat. Ann. §§ 47a-14a to -14h	Conn. Gen. Stat. Ann. § 47a-13
Delaware	Del. Code Ann. tit. 25, § 5308(b)(3)	Del. Code Ann. tit. 25, §§ 5307, 5308
District of Columbia	*Javins v. First Nat'l Realty Corp.*, 428 F.2d 1071 (D.C. Cir. 1970)	No statute
Florida	Fla. Stat. Ann. § 83.60	No statute
Georgia	No statute	No statute
Hawaii	Haw. Rev. Stat. § 521-78	Haw. Rev. Stat. § 521-64
Idaho	No statute	No statute
Illinois	765 Ill. Comp. Stat. §§ 735/2 to /2.2	No statute
Indiana	No statute	No statute
Iowa	Iowa Code Ann. § 562A.24	Iowa Code Ann. § 562A.23
Kansas	Kan. Stat. Ann. § 58-2561	No statute
Kentucky	Ky. Rev. Stat. Ann. § 383.645	Ky. Rev. Stat. Ann. §§ 383.635, 383.640
Louisiana	No statute	La. Civ. Code Ann. art. 2694
Maine	Me. Rev. Stat. Ann. tit. 14, § 6021	Me. Rev. Stat. Ann. tit. 14, § 6026
Maryland	Md. Code Ann. [Real Prop.] §§ 8-211, 8-211.1	No statute
Massachusetts	Mass. Gen. Laws Ann. ch. 239, § 8A	Mass. Gen. Laws Ann. ch. 111, § 127L
Michigan	Mich. Comp. Laws § 125.530	*Rome v. Walker*, 38 Mich. App. 458 (1972); Mich. Comp Laws § 554.139
Minnesota	Minn. Stat. Ann. §§ 504B.215(3)(d), 504B.385	Minn. Stat. Ann § 504B.425
Mississippi	No statute	Miss. Code Ann. § 89-8-15

State Laws on Rent Withholding and Repair and Deduct Remedies (continued)

State	Statute or Case on Rent Withholding	Statute or Case on Repair and Deduct
Missouri	Mo. Ann. Stat. §§ 441.570, 441.580	Mo. Ann. Stat. § 441.234
Montana	Mont. Code Ann. § 70-24-421	Mont. Code Ann. §§ 70-24-406 to -408
Nebraska	Neb. Rev. Stat. §§ 76-1425, -1428	Neb. Rev. Stat. § 76-1427
Nevada	Nev. Rev. Stat. Ann. § 118A.490	Nev. Rev. Stat. Ann. §§ 118A.360, .380
New Hampshire	N.H. Rev. Stat. Ann. § 540:13-d	No statute
New Jersey	N.J. Stat. Ann. §§ 2A:42-85 to -96	*Marini v. Ireland*, 265 A.2d 526 (1970)
New Mexico	N.M. Stat. Ann. § 47-8-27.2	No statute
New York	N.Y. Real Prop. Law § 235-b	*Jangla Realty Co. v. Gravagna*, 447 N.Y.S. 2d 338 (Civ. Ct., Queens County, 1981)
North Carolina	*Surratt v. Newton*, 393 S.E.2d 554 (1987)	No statute
North Dakota	No statute	N.D. Cent. Code § 47-16-13
Ohio	Ohio Rev. Code Ann. § 5321.07	No statute
Oklahoma	Okla. Stat. Ann. tit. 41, § 121	Okla. Stat. Ann. tit. 41, § 121
Oregon	Or. Rev. Stat. § 90.370	Or. Rev. Stat. § 90.365
Pennsylvania	68 Pa. Cons. Stat. Ann. § 250.206; 35 Pa. Cons. Stat. Ann. § 1700-1	*Pugh v. Holmes*, 405 A.2d 897 (1979)
Rhode Island	R.I. Gen. Laws § 34-18-32	R.I. Gen. Laws §§ 34-18-30 to -31
South Carolina	S.C. Code Ann. §§ 27-40-640, -790	No statute
South Dakota	S.D. Codified Laws Ann. § 43-32-9	S.D. Codified Laws Ann. § 43-32-9
Tennessee	Tenn. Code Ann. § 68-111-104	Tenn. Code Ann. § 66-28-502
Texas	No statute	Tex. Prop Code Ann. §§ 92.056, 92.0561
Utah	No statute	No statute
Vermont	Vt. Stat. Ann. tit. 9, § 4458	Vt. Stat. Ann. tit. 9, § 4459
Virginia	Va. Code Ann. §§ 55-248.23 to 55-248.27	No statute
Washington	Wash. Rev. Code Ann. §§ 59.18.110, 59.18.115	Wash. Rev. Code Ann. §§ 59.18.100, .110
West Virginia	*Teller v. McCoy*, 28 S.E. 751 (1978)	No statute
Wisconsin	Wis. Stat. Ann. § 704.07(4)	No statute
Wyoming	Wyo. Stat. § 1-21-1206	No statute

State Laws on Landlord's Access to Rental Property

This is a synopsis of state laws that specify circumstances when a landlord may enter rental premises and the amount of notice required for such entry.

State	State Law Citation	Amount of Notice Required in Non-emergency Situations	To Deal With an Emergency	To Inspect the Premises	To Make Reparis, Alterations, or Improvements	To Show Property to Prospective Tenants or Purchasers	During Tenant's Extended Absence
			Reasons Landlord May Enter				
Alabama	No statute						
Alaska	Alaska Stat. § 34.03.140	24 hours	✔	✔	✔	✔	✔
Arizona	Ariz. Rev. Stat. Ann. § 33-1343	Two days	✔	✔	✔	✔	
Arkansas	No statute						
California	Cal. Civ. Code § 1954	24 hours (48 hours for initial move-out inspection)	✔	✔	✔	✔	
Colorado	No statute						
Connecticut	Conn. Gen. Stat. Ann. §§ 47a-16 to 47a-16a	Reasonable notice	✔	✔	✔	✔	✔
Delaware	Del. Code Ann. tit. 25, §§ 5509, 5510	Two days	✔	✔	✔	✔	✔
District of Columbia	No statute						
Florida	Fla. Stat. Ann. § 83.53	12 hours	✔	✔	✔	✔	✔
Georgia	No statute						
Hawaii	Haw. Rev. Stat. §§ 521-53, 521-70(b)	Two days	✔	✔	✔	✔	✔
Idaho	No statute						
Illinois	No statute						
Indiana	No statute						
Iowa	Iowa Code Ann. §§ 562A.19, 562A.28, 562A.29	24 hours	✔	✔	✔	✔	✔
Kansas	Kan. Stat. Ann. §§ 58-2557, 58-2565	Reasonable notice	✔	✔	✔	✔	✔
Kentucky	Ky. Rev. Stat. Ann. § 383.615	Two days	✔	✔	✔	✔	✔
Louisiana	No statute						
Maine	Me. Rev. Stat. Ann. tit. 14, § 6025	24 hours	✔	✔	✔	✔	
Maryland	No statute						
Massachusetts	Mass. Gen. Laws Ann. ch. 186, § 15B(1)(a)	No notice specified	✔	✔	✔	✔	
Michigan	No statute						
Minnesota	Minn. Stat. Ann. § 504B.211	Reasonable notice	✔	✔	✔	✔	

State Laws on Landlord's Access to Rental Property (continued)

State	State Law Citation	Amount of Notice Required in Nonemergency Situations	To Deal With an Emergency	To Inspect the Premises	To Make Repairs, Alterations, or Improvements	To Show Property to Prospective Tenants or Purchasers	During Tenant's Extended Absence
Mississippi	No statute						
Missouri	No statute						
Montana	Mont. Code Ann. § 70-24-312	24 hours	✔	✔	✔	✔	✔
Nebraska	Neb. Rev. Stat. § 76-1423	One day	✔	✔	✔	✔	✔
Nevada	Nev. Rev. Stat. Ann. § 118A.330	24 hours	✔	✔	✔	✔	
New Hampshire	N.H. Rev. Stat. Ann. § 540-A:3	Notice that is adequate under the circumstances	✔	✔	✔	✔	
New Jersey	No statute						
New Mexico	N.M. Stat. Ann. § 47-8-24	24 hours	✔	✔	✔	✔	✔
New York*	No statute						
North Carolina	No statute						
North Dakota	N.D. Cent. Code § 47-16-07.3	Reasonable notice	✔	✔	✔	✔	
Ohio	Ohio Rev. Code Ann. §§ 5321.04(A)(8), 5321.05(B)	24 hours	✔	✔	✔	✔	
Oklahoma	Okla. Stat. Ann. tit. 41, § 128	One day	✔	✔	✔	✔	
Oregon	Or. Rev. Stat. § 90.322	24 hours	✔	✔	✔	✔	✔
Pennsylvania	No statute						
Rhode Island	R.I. Gen. Laws § 34-18-26	Two days	✔	✔	✔	✔	✔
South Carolina	S.C. Code Ann. § 27-40-530	24 hours	✔	✔	✔	✔	✔
South Dakota	No statute						
Tennessee	Tenn. Code Ann. § 66-28-403	No notice specified	✔	✔	✔	✔	✔
Texas	No statute						
Utah	Utah Code Ann. § 57-22-5(2)(c)	No notice specified	✔		✔		
Vermont	Vt. Stat. Ann. tit. 9, § 4460	48 hours	✔	✔	✔	✔	
Virginia	Va. Code Ann. § 55-248.18	24 hours	✔	✔	✔	✔	✔
Washington	Wash. Rev. Code Ann. § 59.18.150	Two days	✔	✔	✔	✔	
West Virginia	No statute						
Wisconsin	Wis. Stat. Ann. § 704.05(2)	Advance notice	✔	✔	✔	✔	
Wyoming	No statute						

* See *The New York Landlord's Law Book,* by Mary Ann Hallenborg (Nolo), for details on rent stabilization—and rent control—laws and regulations in New York State and New York City.

The Landlord's Duty to Rerent the Premises

State	Landlord must take reasonably prompt steps to rerent	Landlord has no duty to look for and rent to another tenant	Law is unclear or courts have not addressed the issue	State	Landlord must take reasonably prompt steps to rerent	Landlord has no duty to look for and rent to another tenant	Law is unclear or courts have not addressed the issue
Alabama		✔		Montana	✔		
Alaska	✔			Nebraska	✔		
Arizona	✔			Nevada	✔		
Arkansas		✔		New Hampshire			✔
California	✔			New Jersey	✔		
Colorado		✔		New Mexico	✔		
Connecticut	✔			New York			✔
Delaware	✔			North Carolina	✔		
Dist. of Columbia		✔		North Dakota	✔		
Florida		✔		Ohio	✔		
Georgia		✔		Oklahoma	✔		
Hawaii	✔			Oregon	✔		
Idaho	✔			Pennsylvania		✔	
Illinois	✔			Rhode Island	✔		
Indiana	✔			South Carolina	✔		
Iowa	✔			South Dakota			✔
Kansas	✔			Tennessee	✔		
Kentucky	✔			Texas	✔		
Louisiana			✔	Utah	✔		
Maine	✔			Vermont		✔	
Maryland	✔			Virginia	✔		
Massachusetts		✔		Washington	✔		
Michigan			✔	West Virginia			✔
Minnesota		✔		Wisconsin	✔		
Mississippi		✔		Wyoming	✔		
Missouri		✔					

State Laws Prohibiting Landlord Retaliation

This chart lists states that do not allow landlords to retaliate—by eviction, rent hikes, or other negative treatment—when tenants complain about living conditions, exercise legal rights such as the use of repair and deduct statutes and rent withholding, or organize other tenants. Some statutes protect only certain tenant activities or complaints

State	Tenant's Complaint to Landlord or Government Agency	Tenant's Involvement in Tenants' Organization	Tenant's Exercixe of Legal Rights	Retaliation Is Presumed If Negative Reaction by Landlord With Specified Time of Tenant's Act	Statute
Alabama					No statute
Alaska	✔	✔	✔		Alaska Stat. § 34.03.310
Arizona	✔	✔		6 months	Ariz. Rev. Stat. Ann. § 33-1381
Arkansas					No statute
California	✔	✔	✔	180 days	Cal. Civ. Code § 1942.5[1]
Colorado					W.W.G. Corp v. Hughes, 960 P. 2d 720 (1998)
Connecticut	✔	✔	✔	6 months	Conn. Gen. Stat. §§ 47a-20, 47a-33
Delaware	✔	✔	✔	90 days	Del. Code Ann. tit. 25, § 5516
Dist. of Columbia	✔	✔	✔	6 months	D.C. Code § 42-3505.01
Florida	✔	✔			Fla. Stat. Ann. § 83.64
Georgia					No statute
Hawaii	✔		✔		Haw. Rev. Stat. § 521-74
Idaho	✔	✔	✔		Wright v. Brady, 889 P.2d 105 (Ct. App. 1995)
Illinois	✔				765 Ill. Comp. Stat. § 720/1
Indiana					No statute
Iowa	✔	✔		1 year	Iowa Code Ann. § 562A.36
Kansas	✔	✔			Kan. Stat. Ann. § 58-2572
Kentucky	✔	✔		1 year	Ky. Rev. Stat. Ann. § 383.705
Louisiana					No statute
Maine	✔	✔	✔	6 months	4 Me. Rev. Stat. Ann. tit.14, § 6001(3)(4)
Maryland	✔	✔	✔		Md. Code Ann. [Real Prop.] § 8-208.1[2]
Massachusetts	✔	✔	✔	6 months	Mass. Ann. Laws ch. 239, § 2A; ch. 186, § 18
Michigan	✔	✔	✔	90 days	Mich. Comp. Laws § 600.5720
Minnesota	✔		✔	90 days	Minn. Stat. Ann. § 504B.441

[1] (CA) A California tenant may claim the protection of this statute only once in any 12-month period.
[2] (MD) Maryland's statute applies when a retaliatory eviction follows a court case or administrative hearing concerning the tenant's underlying complaint, membership in a tenant organization, or exercise of a legal right. In this situation, a tenant may claim the benefit of Maryland's antiretaliation statute only if the eviction falls within six months of the final determination of the court case or administrative hearing.

State Laws Prohibiting Landlord Retaliation (continued)

State	Tenant's Complaint to Landlord or Government Agency	Tenant's Involvement in Tenants' Organization	Tenant's Exercise of Legal Rights	Retaliation Is Presumed If Negative Reaction by Landlord With Specified Time of Tenant's Act	Statute
Mississippi			✔		Miss. Code Ann. § 89-8-17
Missouri					No statute
Montana	✔	✔		6 months	Mont. Code Ann. § 70-24-431
Nebraska	✔	✔			Neb. Rev. Stat. § 76-1439
Nevada	✔	✔	✔		Nev. Rev. Stat. Ann. § 118A.510
New Hampshire	✔	✔	✔	6 months	N.H. Rev. Stat. Ann. §§ 540:13-a, 540:13-b
New Jersey	✔	✔	✔		N.J. Stat. Ann. §§ 2A:42-10.10, 2A:42-10.12[3]
New Mexico	✔	✔	✔	6 months	N.M. Stat. Ann. § 47-8-39
New York	✔	✔	✔	6 months	N.Y. Real Prop. Law § 223-b
North Carolina	✔	✔	✔	12 months	N.C. Gen. Stat. § 42-37.1
North Dakota					No statute
Ohio	✔	✔			Ohio Rev. Code Ann. § 5321.02
Oklahoma					No statute
Oregon	✔	✔	✔		Or. Rev. Stat. § 90.385
Pennsylvania		✔	✔	6 months (for exercise of legal rights connected with utility service)	68 Pa. Cons. Stat. Ann. §§ 250.205, 399.11
Rhode Island	✔		✔		R.I. Gen. Laws Ann. §§ 34-20-10, 34-20-11
South Carolina	✔				S.C. Code Ann. § 27-40-910
South Dakota	✔	✔	✔	180 days	S.D. Cod. Laws Ann. §§ 43-32-27, 43-32-28
Tennessee	✔		✔		Tenn. Code Ann. §§ 66-28-514, § 68-111-105
Texas	✔		✔	6 months	Tex. Prop. Code § 92.331
Utah	✔				*Building Monitoring Sys. v. Paxton*, 905 P.2d 1215 (Utah 1995)
Vermont	✔	✔			Vt. Stat. Ann. tit. 9, § 4465
Virginia	✔	✔	✔		Va. Code Ann. § 55-248.39
Washington	✔		✔	90 days	Wash. Rev. Code §§ 59.18.240, 59.18.250
West Virginia	✔		✔		*Imperial Colliery Co. v. Fout*, 373 S.E.2d 489 (1988)
Wisconsin	✔		✔		Wis. Stat. § 704.45
Wyoming					No statute

[3] (NJ) If a New Jersey tenant fails to request a renewal of a lease or tenancy within 90 days of the tenancy's expiration (or by the renewal date specified in the lease if longer than 90 days), a landlord may terminate or not renew without a presumption of retaliation.

Selected Rent Control Ordinances

CALIFORNIA

Here is an overview of rent control laws and regulations in Los Angeles, Oakland, San Francisco, and San Jose. For more details and a comprehensive guide to California landlord-tenant law, see *The California Landlord's Law Book: Rights and Responsibilities*, by David Brown, Ralph Warner and Janet Portman (Nolo) and *The California Landlord's Law Book: Evictions*, by David Brown (Nolo).

Los Angeles

Name of Ordinance

Rent Stabilization Ordinance, Los Angeles Municipal Code, Chapter XV, §§ 151.00–155.09.

Adoption Date

4/21/79. Last amended 7/16/2003.

Exceptions

Units constructed (or substantially renovated with at least $10,000 in improvements) after 10/1/78, "luxury" units (defined as 0, 1, 2, 3, or 4+ bedroom units renting for at least $302, $420, $588, $756, or $823, respectively, as of 5/31/78), single-family residences, except where two or more houses are located on the same lot. (§ 151.02.G, M.)

Administration

Los Angeles Housing Department
3550 Wilshire Boulevard, Suite 1500
Los Angeles, CA 90010
Also, 6640 Van Nuys Boulevard
Van Nuys, CA 91405

For information regarding ordinance, call 800-994-4444 or 866-557-7368 (RENT).

Websites: www2.cityofla.org/LAHD/ for information on rent control and www.tenant.net/Other_Areas/Calif/losangel/index.html. For the L.A. Municipal Code, navigate the city's main website at www.ci.la.ca.us. (See front of this appendix.)

Registration

Required.

Vacancy Decontrol

Landlord may charge any rent after a tenant either vacates voluntarily or is evicted for non-payment of rent or breach of a rental agreement provision, or to substantially remodel. (Controls remain if landlord evicts for any other reason, fails to remodel after evicting for that purpose, or terminates or fails to renew a subsidized-housing lease with the city housing authority.) However, once the property is rerented, it is subject to rent control based on the higher rent. (§ 151.06.C.)

Just Cause

Required. (§ 151.09.) Every termination notice must state "the reasons for the termination with specific facts to permit a determination of the date, place, witnesses, and circumstances concerning the reason." (§ 151.09.C.1.) Tenant may not defend unlawful detainer action on the basis of lack of good cause or failure of the notice to state the reason if tenant has disobeyed a pretrial court order requiring him or her to deposit rent into court; see C.C.P. § 1170.5 and *Green v. Superior Court* (1974) 10 Cal. 3d 616. (§ 151.09.E.). State law requires use of a 60-day termination notice of month-to-month tenancy, instead of a 30-day notice, for this city, if the tenant has occupied the premises for a year or more.

Other Features

Tenant may defend on the basis that the landlord failed to register the property in accordance with the ordinance. (§ 151.09.F.)

Oakland

Name of Ordinance

"Ordinance Establishing a Residential Rent Arbitration Board," Oakland Municipal Code, Title 8, Ch. 8.22, §§ 8.22.010-8.22.190. See also Title 8, Ch. 8.22, §§ 8.22.300-8.22.480.

Adoption Date

10/7/80. Last amended 10/2003.

Exceptions

Units constructed after 1/18/84, buildings "substantially rehabilitated" at cost of 50% of that of new construction, as determined by Chief Building Inspector. (§ 8.22.030.)

Administration

Rent Adjustment Program
250 Frank H. Ogawa Plaza
Oakland, CA 94612
510-238-3721
FAX: 510-238-3691
Website: www.ci.oakland.ca.us or www.oaklandnet.com. Choose the Municipal Code and go to Title 8, Chapter 8.22; or, choose "Rent Ordinance" and click "Go."

Registration

Not required.

Vacancy Decontrol

Landlord may charge any rent after a tenant vacates voluntarily or is evicted for nonpayment of rent. If tenant otherwise vacates involuntarily, landlord may not increase the rent for 24 months.

On eviction for reasons other than nonpayment of rent, ordinance allows increase of up to 12%, depending on rent increases over previous 12 months.

Once property is rerented, it is subject to rent control based on the higher rent.

Just Cause

Under a separate "Just Cause for Eviction" ordinance (Measure EE), enacted 11/5/2002, landlords may terminate a month-to-month rental agreement (or refuse to renew a lease) only when the tenant has failed to pay the rent (or has violated another important lease term), refused to enter into a written renewal of a rental agreement or lease, caused substantial damage, disturbed the peace and quiet of other tenants, engaged in illegal activities, or refused entry to the landlord when properly asked. Landlords may also terminate rental agreements or not renew leases when they want to live in the unit themselves (or intend it for a close family member), or to substantially renovate the unit. (See Municipal Code Title 8, Ch. 22 §§ 8.22.300-8.22.480.)

Other Features

Rent increase notices must be in a form prescribed by Section 8.22.070(H)(1), which requires tenant be notified of right to petition rent board. All Tenants, on moving in, must be provided a notice informing of their rights under the ordinance. (§ 8.22.060.)

Landlord evicting to "rehabilitate" the property (presumably to obtain permanent exemption from controls) must obtain building permit before eviction.

San Francisco

Name of Ordinance

Residential Rent Stabilization and Arbitration Ordinance, San Francisco Administrative Code, Chapter 37.

Adoption Date

6/79. Last amended 5/16/2003.

Exceptions

Units constructed after 6/79; buildings over 50 years old and "substantially rehabilitated" since 6/79. (§ 37.2 (p).)

Administration

Residential Rent Stabilization and
Arbitration Board
25 Van Ness Avenue, Suite 320
San Francisco, CA 94102
415-252-4602, 415-252-4600 (recorded info)
FAX 415-252-4699
Website: www.ci.sf.ca.us/rentbd or www.sfgov.org/site/rentboard_index.htm. Municipal Code/Administrative Code is available from the city official site, www.ci.sf.ca.us. Rent control laws (in superior format) and regulations are available from rent board site.

Registration

Not required.

Vacancy Decontrol

Landlord may charge any rent after a tenant vacates voluntarily or is evicted for cause. Once property is rerented for a year, it is subject to rent control based on the higher rent. (§ 37.3(a).)

Just Cause

Required. Every termination notice must state "the grounds under which possession is sought" and must advise the tenant that advice regarding the notice is available from the Board. (§ 37.9.)

Other Features

Tenant or Board may sue landlord, following either unsuccessful eviction attempt or successful eviction based on falsified reason, for treble damages and attorney's fees. (§ 37.9(e).) Landlord must file copy of tenancy termination notice (except Three-Day Notice to Pay Rent or Quit) with rent board within ten days after it is served on the tenant. (§ 37.9(c).)

San Jose

Name of Ordinance

San Jose Rental Dispute Mediation and Arbitration Ordinance, San Jose Municipal Code, Title 17, Chapter 17.23, §§ 17.23.010-17.23.770.

Adoption Date

7/7/79. Last amended 7/1/2003.

Exceptions

Units constructed after 9/7/79, single-family residences, duplexes, townhouses, and condominium units. (§ 17.23.150.)

Administration

San Jose Rental Rights and Referrals Program
4 N. Second Street, Suite 600
San Jose, CA 95113
408-277-5431
Website: www.ci.san-jose.ca.us. This is the general city site, which provides no rent control information. The telephone menu, however, at 408-277-5431, provides much useful information. Municipal Code is accessible. Rent control portions are in Title 17, Chapter 17.23.

Registration

Required.

Vacancy Decontrol

Landlord may charge any rent after a tenant vacates voluntarily or is evicted following Three-Day Notice to Pay Rent or Quit or other breach of the rental agreement. However, once the new rent for a vacated unit is established by the landlord and the property is rerented, it is subject to rent control based on the higher rent. (§ 17.23.190.)

Just Cause

Not required. Notice requirements and unlawful detainer procedures are governed solely by state law.

Other

All tenants, on moving in, must be provided a notice informing of their rights under the ordinance. (§ 17.23.030.) Rent increase notices must notify tenant of right to petition, time limits, and the city rent programs's address and phone number (§ 17.23.270.)

In addition, ordinance requires that 90-day notice of termination be given to a tenant of month-to-month tenancy that's lasted over a year, or a 60-day notice if served with an offer to arbitrate. We believe this provision is invalid as superseded by recent state law allowing a 60-day notice without an offer to arbitrate.

Important: Copies of Notices to Vacate must be sent to the city. (§ 17.23.760.)

Other States

District of Columbia
Washington, D.C.

Ordinance Adoption Date

7/17/1985 (Rental Housing Act of 1985, District of Columbia Code §§ 42-3501.01 and following); substantial amendment April 2001, D.C. Law 13-281.

Administration

Housing Regulation Authority; Rental Housing Commission, 941 North Capitol St., N.E., Washington, DC 20002, 202-442-4610. For details on rules and procedures, see http://dcra.dc.gov.

New Jersey
Newark

Ordinance Adoption Date

11/20/1973 (Title 15, Housing Chapters 9A and 9B). Last amended December 1996.

Administration

Rent Control Board, Room 113, 920 Broad Street, Newark, NJ 07102. For information regarding ordinance, 973-733-3675 or www.ci.newark.nj.us/municipal_services/all_services/housing_property.html.

Maryland
Takoma Park

Ordinance Adoption Date

1980. (Takoma Park Rent Stabilization Law. Chapter 6, Housing Article 5, Rent Stabilization.) Latest amendment 4/23/2004.

Administration

Office on Landlord-Tenant Services, Housing Department, 7500 Maple Avenue, Takoma Park, MD 20912. 301-891-7216. For details see http://207.176.62.2/ecd/housing/documents/rent.html.

New York

More than one million rental units in dozens of localities across New York State, including New York City, are subject to either "rent stabilization" or "rent control"—the principal forms of rent regulation in New York. Rent laws and regulations control far more than how much rent a landlord may charge. They also govern security deposits, required services, sublet rights, landlord's right to access, how and under what circumstances the landlord can end a tenancy, and more. For complete details on these rules, see *The New York Landlord's Law Book,* by Mary Ann Hallenborg, published by Nolo. It is available at bookstores and public libraries and may be ordered directly from Nolo at www.nolo.com, or 800-728-3555. See also New York State Division of Housing and Community Renewal, Rent Administration, www.dhcr.state.ny.us/ora/ora.htm.

INDEX

Repair-and-deduct remedy, 2/20, 7/15,
7/21–22, 11/3, Appendix 2/11–12
Repairs and maintenance, 7/2–30
asbestos problem, 7/2, 7/7–8, 7/22
emergency repairs, 7/12
entry by landlord to make, 8/5
landlord's responsibilities, 7/4, 7/5, 7/10,
7/25–27
lead problem, 7/2, 7/7, 7/22, 7/23
lease/rental agreement provisions on,
2/12–13
major vs. minor, 7/5–7
options if repairs not made, 7/14–24, 7/28,
7/29–30
requesting repairs, 7/12–14, 7/19, 7/27–29,
7/30
security deposit withholding for, 4/4, 10/2–3
tenant's responsibilities, 7/11–12, 7/27, 7/30
tips on, 7/2–3, 7/30
Residency status, requests for proof of, 1/5,
5/5
Retaliation, 11/2–8
defined, 11/5
for habitability complaints, 11/3, 11/8
nonrenewal of lease as, 3/9, 11/8
rent increases, 3/11, 3/13–14, 11/5, 11/6–7
for rent withholding, 7/16, 11/3, 11/4, 11/8
responding to, 11/5–8
state laws, 11/2, 11/3–4, 11/8, Appendix
2/16–17
termination of tenancy as, 3/9, 11/5, 11/6,
11/8
Returned check fees, 3/7
Rights to privacy. *See* Privacy rights
Roomers, 6/4, 6/15–16
See also Subtenants
Roommates, 6/2–16
adding, 6/12, 6/13–16, 12/3

agreements with, 6/6–9, 6/16
defined, 6/4
getting rid of, 6/5, 6/10
if a roommate leaves, 6/11–13
legal terminology, 6/3–4
limit on number of, 1/4, 2/27
questions about relationship between, 1/7
resolving disputes with, 6/10, 13/5
See also Cotenants; Subtenants

S

Safety inspectors, 8/9
Sale of building
security deposits, 4/9
showing property, 8/6
San Francisco
Project Open Door (SPCA), 2/25
rent control ordinance, 12/8, Appendix
2/20
San Jose rent control ordinance, 12/2,
Appendix 2/21
Savings clauses, 2/30
Section 8 housing, 5/11
Security deposits, 4/2–9, 10/2–8
avoiding problems with, 10/6–8
dollar limits, 3/12, 4/3
if breaking lease, 9/14, 9/15
if building is sold, 4/9
if landlord declares bankruptcy, 4/8
increases in amount of, 3/12, 4/4, 6/15
interest on, 4/7–8, 12/8
last month's rent and, 2/11, 4/5–6, 4/9, 9/2
lease/rental agreement provisions on, 2/11
legal uses of, 4/4–5, 10/2–3
letter explaining tenant's cleaning plans,
10/7–8
negotiating amount and payment of, 4/3–4

T

Remember:

Little publishers have big ears.
We really listen to you.

Take 2 Minutes & Give Us Your 2 cents

Your comments make a big difference in the development and revision of Nolo books and software. Please take a few minutes and register your Nolo product—and your comments—with us. Not only will your input make a difference, you'll receive special offers available only to registered owners of Nolo products on our newest books and software. Register now by:

PHONE
1-800-728-3555

FAX
1-800-645-0895

EMAIL
cs@nolo.com

or **MAIL** us
this registration card

fold here

Registration Card

NAME _____ DATE _____

ADDRESS _____

_____

CITY _____ STATE _____ ZIP _____

PHONE _____ EMAIL _____

WHERE DID YOU HEAR ABOUT THIS PRODUCT? _____

WHERE DID YOU PURCHASE THIS PRODUCT? _____

DID YOU CONSULT A LAWYER? (PLEASE CIRCLE ONE)   YES   NO   NOT APPLICABLE

DID YOU FIND THIS BOOK HELPFUL?   (VERY)   5   4   3   2   1   (NOT AT ALL)

COMMENTS _____

_____

_____

WAS IT EASY TO USE?   (VERY EASY)   5   4   3   2   1   (VERY DIFFICULT)

We occasionally make our mailing list available to carefully selected companies whose products may be of interest to you.

❑ If you do not wish to receive mailings from these companies, please check this box.

❑ You can quote me in future Nolo promotional materials.
   Daytime phone number _____.

RENT 4.0

Nolo
in the
NEWS

"Nolo helps lay people perform legal tasks without the aid—or fees—of lawyers."

—USA TODAY

Nolo books are ..."written in plain language, free of legal mumbo jumbo, and spiced with witty personal observations."

—ASSOCIATED PRESS

"...Nolo publications...guide people simply through the how, when, where and why of law."

—WASHINGTON POST

"Increasingly, people who are not lawyers are performing tasks usually regarded as legal work... And consumers, using books like Nolo's, do routine legal work themselves."

—NEW YORK TIMES

"...All of [Nolo's] books are easy-to-understand, are updated regularly, provide pull-out forms...and are often quite moving in their sense of compassion for the struggles of the lay reader."

—SAN FRANCISCO CHRONICLE

- - - - - - - - - - - - - - fold here - - - - - - - - - - - - - - - -

**950 Parker Street
Berkeley, CA 94710-9867**

Attn: RENT 4.0